HANDBOOK OF PROGRESSIVE GYMNASTICS

Tom De Carlo

Coach of Gymnastics
Queens (N. Y.) College

Prentice-Hall, Inc.
Englewood Cliffs, N. J.

Handbook of Progressive Gymnastics

Handbook of Progressive Gymnastics,
by Tom De Carlo
© 1963 by Prentice-Hall, Inc.
Englewood Cliffs, N.J.

Library of Congress Catalog Card Number: 63-21441

Third Printing . . . February, 1966

PRINTED IN THE UNITED STATES OF AMERICA
38066–B C

To
Rene J. Kern
a
Dedicated Teacher
and
Sincere Friend

Preface

During my association with gymnastics both as
teacher and performer, I have come to appreciate and to respect the activity for its contribution to the development of the "whole
person." This thought, along with the desire
to share my teaching experiences, gradually
developed into the writing of this book.

Opinions and suggestions of many gymnastic teachers, especially those on the Junior-

Senior High School and collegiate levels, were solicited to acquire a true cross section of the type of gymnastic system most needed by teachers. The majority agreed that such a system should include a series of continuous skills aimed at various grade levels and brief but accurate descriptions of these skills in simple nomenclature with accompanying illustrations to allow for teacher-pupil interpretation. It should also recommend a safety procedure that would encompass correct spotting and assisting methods and provide safety hints for other vital aspects of the program. Finally, the system should include means of promoting gymnastic programs to school administrators and an accurate historical and bibliographical account for further reference.

In this text I have endeavored to fulfill these requests. The survey was instrumental in assisting in the preparation of the progressive system and only after many trial and error sessions was the final handbook adopted. The book is divided into six classified levels of progressions, (Beginner, Novice, Intermediate, Junior, Advanced and Senior) and, because of its nature, the application is most effective at the secondary level (grades 7-12).

It also contains over 300 individual gymnastic skills with major emphasis on the "all-around" program. Each skill's action is thoroughly described and presented with sound teaching techniques.

The discussion on nomenclature is presented to help communication by describing a simplified terminology that has as its nucleus four basic positions. Further, the chapter dealing with safety suggests safeguards for all phases of the instructional program with primary stress on spotting suggestions for every skill throughout the text. There is a portion devoted to the care and prevention of the athletic injuries most associated with apparatus activities. Also incorporated are various suggestions aimed at overcoming the administrative red tape that usually accompanies the formulation and promotion of a gymnastic program.

The handbook has been designed to serve as both a text and a reference for anyone engaged in gymnastics. The many progressive drawings and photographs enable the instructor to present an activity without having actively engaged in that particular skill.

The skills and procedures in this book are presented in their actual teaching sequence, and the unit plans have been prepared to enable the coach to concentrate on ease of teaching and understanding, rather than on complexity of planning and interpretation.

In an effort to further assist the instructor, the handbook contains a system for teaching gymnastics to groups of all sizes, abilities and body types; recommendations for lesson plan time splits, from the taking of the attendance to the time of the shower; and discusses the training of squad leaders and a preclass conditioning drill. For those whose budgetary allowances do not provide for a complete set of apparatus, the section devoted to promotional activities suggests how to build inexpensive but adequate equipment.

Various portions of progressive gymnastics, especially the historical phase, represent in part the writings and findings of others. However, the historical interpretation of gymnastics which is presented reveals many significant attitudes and occurrences that have directly influenced the trend of modern gymnastics. In this complex world, such knowledge can help us to understand the present and to learn new and improved techniques. Only in such a manner will gymnastics continue to progress and students improve.

Acknowledgments

The author is sincerely indebted to *Rene (Frenchie) Kern*, of the Brooklyn Central Young Men's Christian Association, for introducing the writer to the sport of gymnastics and for his unselfishness in sharing his time, his talents and especially himself, to the cause of helping young men; to *Leslie J. Judd*, Professor Emeritus (Springfield College), for his constant inspiration and professional leadership, both as a friend and as a teacher; to *Lyle Welser*, of Georgia Tech University, for his helping to crystallize the author's thinking of the Progressive Gymnastic Program; to *Sidney Birnbach* of the Yonkers (New York) Board of Education, for his personal interest and continuous direction in helping the author to establish himself in Physical Education; to *Herman Masin*, of *Scholastic Coach Magazine*, for his encouragement in the writing of parts of this manuscript; to *Frances Hoffman*, of Queens College (New York), for assisting in the interpretation and application of the anatomical and physiological aspects of the hand-book; to *William Buffa*, National Chairman of the Young Men's Christian Association Gymnastic Committee, for his assistance in contributing parts of the text's nomenclature; to *Don Tonry*, a superb gymnast and personal friend, who so expertly provided the drawings along with their mechanical analysis contained in *Progressive Gymnastics*; and to *my wife* and *three sons*, who were extremely patient during the trying times that accompany such a work, who served as a constant beacon whose rays were symbolic of love, kindness and understanding.

Tom De Carlo

Contents

Chapter V
Beginner Skills, 57

Chapter VI
Novice Skills, 77

Chapter VII
Intermediate Skills, 99

Chapter VIII
Junior Skills, 117

Chapter XII
A History of Gymnastics to the 19th Century, 201

Chapter XIII
Gymnastics in Modern Europe, 211

Chapter XIV
Gymnastics in the United States, 219

Selected Bibliography, 233

Index, 235

The Scope

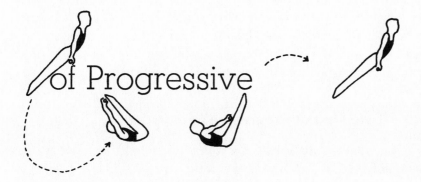

of Progressive

Gymnastics

1

Progressive gymnastics, through its all-around program, is concerned with the development of the total individual. As teachers of physical education, we are primarily interested in activities that will motivate the individual to think about his own physical development objectives. These activities should utilize constructive physical action and provide wholesome physical experiences. If properly motivated, the student will perform the same activities in his leisure time. Hopefully, then, a program of progressive gymnastics will have a place in all facets of the student's life and aid in his total growth and health.

In evaluating the reasons for installing a program of progressive gymnastics, one must understand the program as a whole. The basic needs of the individual must be considered and the role gymnastics can play in fulfilling them clarified. The availability of facilities must be related to the worth of the different activities to decide how extensive a program must be installed. Once the answers to these questions have been arrived at, the groundwork for putting a program of progressive gymnastics into being will be established.

Basic Aims of Progressive Gymnastics

The aims of progressive gymnastics should be embodied in *unattainable* goals. As Browning wrote:

> One's reach should exceed one's grasp
> Or what's a heaven for?

Progressive gymnastics should also aspire beyond its grasp and thus ensure a future of progress. The aims are as follows:

1. To increase and maintain total fitness for American youth. Physical fitness goes hand in hand with moral, mental, and emotional fitness.
2. To increase the degree of student mastery in the basic elements of gymnastic activity; to serve as a foundation for the wide variety of skills needed on more advanced levels of competition.
3. To aid the gymnastic instructor in teaching and testing the basic elements of gymnastic activity.

General Objectives

Our objectives have been evaluated as worthwhile since they have measured up to the standard of the basic aims.

There are three essential objectives to be achieved by progressive gymnastics.

The *first* is *physical fitness*. The development that these dynamic activities add to to one's total body development is equalled by few other activities. Strength, stamina, coordination, agility, and flexibility are just a few of their rewards. These qualities leave lasting impressions.

The *second* objective is *social efficiency*. Through its individualized nature, gymnastics aids in developing one's personality and emotional well-being to an extent much greater than that normally associated with sports. It gives one an inner feeling of self-confidence and sureness. It also serves as a definite outlet to those in need of such an activity. Through its essentials of spotting and harmonious cooperation, one develops a sense of trust in and need for his fellow man. Words cannot describe the feeling of accomplishment when a particular stunt or routine is achieved. This sensation of self-satisfaction is unsurpassable.

The *third* objective is *recreational competency*. One of the most successful recreational outgrowths of an apparatus program is competitive and exhibitional gymnastics. Various *Turnvereins*, Y.M.C.A.'s, Athletic Clubs, schools and colleges utilize this last objective to a high degree. Exhibitional and apparatus training is one sport where co-educational activity can exist. Through the medium of routines and dances, leisure-time activity can be spent in a very pleasing and worthwhile atmosphere.

These activities are predominately practiced in gymnasia, but can also be practiced at various places of recreation, such as beaches, picnics, and lyceums. With the proper leadership and attitude, a performer, by utilizing the essential aims and objectives of gymnastics, can force his magnetic qualities into the lives of both spectators and performers.

Meeting Individual Needs

Another aspect of the progressive gymnastics program deals with meeting individual needs. Because the activity lends itself to an individualistic approach to learning and because it is comprised of progressive self-testing skills, by its own nature it becomes a major contributor to individual needs, namely: BELONGING or group accept-ance; ACHIEVEMENT or accomplishment of particular skills; SHARING AND SELF-RESPECT or self-expression through routine planning and deciding its true value through individual and group opinions. Other attributes are: HUMILITY in victory and GRACIOUSNESS in defeat; UNDER-STANDING or the natural inquisitiveness of children to ask questions and to "probe" details of individual skills or whole activities.

To summarize, progressive gymnastics provides the student with excellent opportunities for learning, related to the interpretation of his environment, himself, and his associates. He gains insight into his own nature and that of his fellow man.

Program Depends on Adequate Facilities

A very important consideration is availability of facilities. Unfor-tunately, all of us are not equipped with the necessary facilities to conduct an adequate gymnastics program. However, with a little pre-planning and some imagination, a satisfactory program can be main-tained until the necessary facilities are secured.

Heavy apparatus such as parallel bars and side horses, have to be purchased outright. If the budget prohibits the purchase of other basic equipment, certain items may be obtained from the local hard-ware store and lumber yard and assembled by the school's industrial arts department. These would include certain ring attachments, spot-ting "rigs," vaulting box, beat board, and parallels.

Under no circumstances, when attempting to cut corners, should a department sacrifice individual safety. This phase of the program should always be given the highest priority, as one serious accident could not only endanger a student's well-being, but it could also efface your entire gymnastics program.

Worth of Different Activities

Of great significance in organizing progressive gymnastics, is the worth of different activities. Few activities on the American sports scene are as conducive to growth of all the basic qualities underlying total fitness as is gymnastics—when judiciously applied. These are the qualities made visible in the performance of an activity in which there is a smoothness of muscular action, a conscious economy of energy, and a performance with grace and finesse. These are qualities significantly essential in the desire for a richly active life, a desire which modern civilization tends to curb rather than to encourage.

Nature of Progressive Gymnastics

Progressive gymnastics, in essence, has been organized to acquaint both teacher and pupil with artistic gymnastics. The progressions are divided into six individual units: Beginner, Novice, Intermediate, Junior, Advanced and Senior. Each of these units represents one season of skills to be learned. Therefore, a boy participating at the Beginner level is assumed to have had no previous experience in the all-around gymnastic program. Contrarily, a boy participating at the Intermediate level is assumed to have had two seasons of experience (Beginner and Novice) in the all-around gymnastic program.

It is strongly recommended that a boy not start the all-around program until he is 11 or 12 years of age or upon entering the seventh grade (it is assumed that once a boy starts progressive gymnastics he will continue its chronological order until completed). By no means does this imply that the program has no application to younger children. Individual parts of the Beginner, Novice and even the Intermediate Units (example, Long Horse, Tumbling, etc.) would be very applicable to primary grade children. However, to plan an all-around gymnastic program at this time would not be pedagogically or medically sound because time allotments (in schools) during these years in physical education are too short (30 minutes is usually maximum), the child's interest span is very limited and the individual's physiological structure is not mature enough for the total activity.

On the collegiate level, the programs in physical education can easily make the adjustment by grouping students according to their previous years of experience in the progressive gymnastics program.

In an effort to develop individual total growth, the program is centered around the all-around gymnastics program whose activities include: Floor Exercise, Long Horse, Side Horse, Horizontal Bar, Parallel Bars, and Still Rings. I have included Tumbling and Rope Climb because it was felt that these activities contain many qualities that can constitute significant carry-over value in the remaining programs. The developing of one's self-confidence, equilibrium, and acrobatic skills through tumbling activities, can be correlated with many movements engaged in on the apparatus and especially in the floor exercise.

A primary factor essential for the successful execution of gymnastic skills is strength in the arms and shoulders above that of the average individual. Rope Climb was adopted to progressive gymnastics because it was felt that a climbing activity would increase upper body strength and serve as an excellent warm-up activity.

Flying Rings and Rebound Tumbling have been omitted because the sport of gymnastics (whose rules for the conducting of gymnastic competitions are promulgated by the Amateur Athletic Union) does not include these activities as part of the all-around program. It is the opinion of prominent teachers of gymnastics that Still Rings and the remaining gymnastic activities compensate for the omission of Flying Rings and Rebound tumbling.

It must be remembered that the success of any program depends upon its teacher. The gymnastic program should be taught to provide the student with wholesome physical experiences which are meaningful enough so that he can use these or similar activities during his leisure time. Although actual time spent in the physical education class is relatively short, the instructor can stimulate the students in such a manner that they will pursue the skills in their spare time. The child will thus have received gymnastics in its proper form. In order to make the individual think, we have to present part of the program in lecture form. This can be accomplished by short discussions about the day's lesson before getting into the actual practicing of the activity. Through a better understanding of the child we can reach him in his present stage of development and can devise ways of motivating him to accept the program. The degree to which the students practice gymnastics will depend upon our presentation of knowledge of the subject matter and the attitude that we can inculcate into their thinking.

Values of Progressive Gymnastics

1. Gymnastics contributes to the development of all component

parts of individual physical fitness which includes: strength, endurance, agility, flexibility, balance, speed, and power.

2. Gymnastics helps to promote good muscle tone in the arms and legs which provides for improved circulation.

3. Gymnastics aids in counteracting and even preventing nervous stress and strain. It has been said that an hour's workout will do more good to an unhappy but otherwise healthy person than all the medicine and psychology in the world.

4. Gymnastics provides an atmosphere which is conducive to optimum growth and development. The all-around program allows for organic stimulation and maintenance of individual health.

5. Gymnastic activity maintains a correlation between time and space. A kinesthetic sense is developed within the person which the student, when executing a variety of somersaults, twists and turns, develops a keen perception as to his exact position during the execution of a stunt and is thus able to complete the movement with the utmost safety.

6. Gymnastics stimulates finer neuro-muscular coordination which allows for a well coordinated and supple individual.

7. Gymnastics offers remedial exercises to physically handicapped individuals. Through a series of prescribed corrective exercises the student can not only remedy his physical defects but enjoy a very exciting program.

8. Gymnastics assists in developing a symmetrical looking physique. This mesomorphic quality can have very favorable implications for one's social acceptance.

9. Gymnastics tends to stimulate and to develop such mental states as daring and courage, perseverance, decisiveness, initiative, self-confidence, and presence of mind. The individual is called upon to plan his sequence of movements, overcome possible indecisions, and then act.

10. Gymnastics enhances such qualities as personal improvement and creative expression. Each new stunt or routine that is accomplished in class makes one more appreciative of the true meaning of such terms as continuity, balance and beauty. These qualities provide for an expressional creativity within one's own physical and mental capacities which leads to a personal satisfaction second to none.

11. Gymnastics entertains many experiences which produce desirable social and ethical behavior. The developing of poise, honesty, self-control and respect for one's fellow student all contribute to this value. The practicing of "waiting your turn" before entering upon the apparatus and learning right from wrong through trial and error all contribute to the philosophy of "there are no gains without pains" in life.

12. Gymnastic skills help condition a person to such a degree that there is a tremendous carry-over value to other sports. Many divers and track and field performers, to mention a few, utilize gymnastic training for personal gain in these related sports.

13. Gymnastics can serve as a worthy recreational activity. The inter-personal relationships that are contained within this sport can be seen in exhibitional gymnastics and plain old "family kabitzin."

14. Gymnastics develops leadership ability within an individual. This quality can serve as a basis for future engagements in life as well as to provide valuable assistance in the required physical education program as squad leaders, and demonstrators.

15. Gymnastics, because it is such an individualized activity, can be used as a self-testing activity, which in turn can serve as a basis for one's final grade in the physical education program.

The value of progressive gymnastics may very well be summarized by a verse which the poet John Dryden wrote to a kinsman in 1680. One of the stanzas in that letter went as follows:

> By chase our fathers earned their food,
> Toil strung [improved] the nerves and purified the blood,
> But we their sons, a pampered race of men,
> Are dwindled down to three score years and ten.
> Better to hunt in fields for health unbought,
> Than fee the doctor for a nauseous draught.
> The wise for cure on exercise depend,
> God never made his work for man to mend.

Techniques 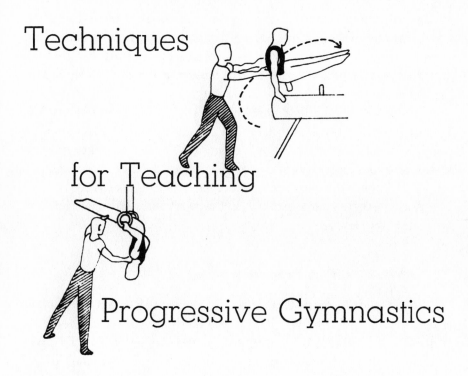 for Teaching Progressive Gymnastics

II

The teaching of progressive gymnastics is chiefly in the realm of motor learning. These voluntary movements that determine the degree of execution of any given skill are dependent on sound teaching procedures and proper training techniques.

Today's instructors are dealing with a multitude of individual personalities; therefore, one must always be ready to show them respect if one is to command it. The psychological factor plays a very important role in the teaching success of any gymnastics program. Pupils want someone that they can look to for direction, whether it be for one's teaching sincerity or for one's superior skill in performance. The instructor who exhibits an enthusiasm towards and knowledge of the activity has an excellent opportunity to motivate his students to participate in such a manner that enjoyment and success will be inevitable.

In gymnastics the best performer is not always the best teacher. The art of good teaching is achieved through years of experience. A competitor may know all of the fundamentals and mechanics of gymnastics activity; however, if he cannot translate this knowlege into simple and concise terms, sound teaching will not take place.

A tangible teaching method is the most essential tool that any instructor can possess.

Whole vs. Part Procedure

In any debate on method, there is always the question of *whole* or *part* methods of teaching. The whole method signifies the teaching of a unit as a whole until complete mastery is achieved. The part method signifies the breaking down of each skill into simple and concise units and learning them, one by one, in proper sequence, until the whole movement is properly executed.

In teaching gymnastics, you should utilize the different methods according to the situation. The progressive system has been planned to meet individual needs and abilities; therefore, individuals should plan each lesson with an open approach rather than with a "set" pattern. You must be flexible. For example, if a student has the ability to perform a newly introduced skill in its entirety, why should his progress be suppressed by requiring him to practice individual components of the whole move for the sake of standard procedure? Obviously, he does not require this type of breakdown. Conversely, if a pupil cannot grasp a new move in its entirety, rather than retard his progress by submitting him to practice a skill beyond his present realm of difficulty, he should be introduced to the individual parts that apparently are necessary in his particular situation. Since individual situations cannot be accurately calculated, the final choice of method is up to the discretion of the teacher in charge.

Fundamental Approach

Basically, instruction usually proceeds from the *psychological* to the *logical*, from the *whole* to the *part*. This method of teaching accompanies a fundamental instructional approach; one that should be employed with each progressive lesson. The procedure entails: *(1)* explanation of skill by the instructor; *(2)* demonstration of skill by the instructor, student leader or by audio-visual assistance; *(3)* participation in the learning of the skill by the student; *(4)* correction of pupil's execution of skills; *(5)* standard of performance or testing pupil's skill for a particular exercise, or a series of exercises (the testing phase does not necessarily have to be included with each daily lesson since most plans do not call for testing on a day-to-day basis).

Let us further relate this approach to an instructional situation. The skill is explained to the class by the instructor. He may be assisted by a planned audio-visual aid program such as the diagrams contained within this text, animated models, or loop films. This explanation is accompanied by the student's ability to psychologically understand the instructor's explanation. (It should be noted that the student's "psychological moment," or that moment when his mind is most willing to accept a fact, is dependent on the instructor's ability to create an atmosphere that is conducive to the learning situation.) Certain students, at this time, will be able to convert this explanation into a logical sequence; others will need further demonstrations.

Demonstration and Comprehension

The skill is then demonstrated, clarifying the finer points of execution. At this stage, the student would normally make the logical association by interpreting to himself how he would go about executing the particular skill. His performance of that movement would be subject to his individual understanding and interpretating as well as to his motor ability.

Individual students will make individual interpretations of the logical sequence of execution. At this time they are given the opportunity to apply their thinking by participating in the practicing of the skill. The degree to which the pupil can make a motor translation of his interpretation will determine to what extent the accompanying whole-or-part method of learning is employed. The very concept of progressive gymnastics makes it possible for teachers to approach each new stunt from the whole method of instruction. If the pupil cannot grasp the skill in its entirety, then and only then should the part method be employed—approaching each skill from a positive point of view. Explain the move in a simple and concise manner and with the attitude that the maneuver is fairly simple and rather easy to learn. However, one should be very careful not to confuse haphazardness with simplicity.

In correcting the student's performance, the instructor has the option of suggesting to the pupil, according to his execution of skill, that the move be broken down into component parts which would enhance quicker learning, or that the exercise be further continued in its entirety until a desirable degree of execution is achieved. This method of instruction should be continuously guided by a practical and individualistic approach; one that has shown to be very effective in progressive gymnastics.

Procedures Used for Group Participation

The three most common procedures used in conducting gymnastics classes are: *(1)* the Squad Procedure, *(2)* the Class Procedure, and *(3)* the Free Play Procedure. Progressive gymnastics utilizes not one but all three methods. Difference in one's situation, students, equipment and ability to teach will determine the immediate procedure.

Squad Procedure

In most instances the squad method will prove to be the most successful. This is the process of dividing a class into various groups and having them spend part of the period at a particular station. When the instructor signals, all squads rotate to the next event. A clockwise rotation will allow for better class organization since the pupils find it simple to follow and easy to remember, thus enabling the instructor to have a well organized class at all times.

A varying range of somato-types within a class could possibly offer a multitude of shortcomings to the group as a whole due to the individual's lack or increase of motor ability and physical maturity. A sound teaching technique should be incorporated to make allowance for the different abilities that comprise any given class. Therefore, when utilizing the squad method, homogeneous grouping should be exercised. Separation according to body types has proven to be very successful in the teaching of progressive gymnastics. The *mesomorphic* (muscular) and *ectomorphic* (thin) students will in most instances acquire skills more rapidly than the *endomorphic* (obese) students. By making this group distinction one is insuring that the individual squads will be free to progress according to their own abilities.

It is very discouraging for a skillful individual to be mixed in with slow learners. The situation somehow reduces his enthusiasm, thus inhibiting his progress. On the other hand, it is equally discouraging as well as embarrassing for an unskilled individual to be mixed in with those possessing superior abilities. The happy medium is very desirable.

On the other hand, if it is apparent that a particular individual, in spite of his somato-type is not homogeneously grouped, he can always be placed elsewhere.

If you resort to the rotating squad method, you must carefully weigh such factors as class size and time allotment when organizing a lesson plan. Normally, a squad of six to eight students should spend a minimum of 10 minutes at each gymnastic station in order to achieve basic satisfaction from the exercises. The classes should be divided into squads of eight to correspond to the number of events contained within the progressive program. If you find that this type of division spreads the class too thin, it is suggested that tumbling be consolidated with free calisthenics and that the class climb the ropes as a pre-class warm-up.

Periods are usually 45 minutes long. Actual participation is allotted approximately 20 minutes—thereby giving each squad one change (starting at one event and changing to another). Sixty minutes as well as double periods would allow for two changes (*see* Table 1). The majority of students will find three events to be their maximum load in any given period. The instructor in planning his rotation should make certain that each squad covers the exercises at all stations whether it takes two, three or even four lessons, before they repeat an event. It is a good practice to post the rotation schedule for the semester on the bulletin board to make each squad aware of its lesson for the day.

Class Procedure

There are certain instances when the Class and Free Play techniques will prove to be very valuable. The class method may be employed for instruction in free calisthenics. This activity requires a large area and should be taught after the conditioning exercises. This will eliminate the reorganizing of groups into large areas and will insure the class of receiving a thorough warm-up. This method is also very valuable with small groups and mass equipment.

Free Play Procedure

Every so often it would be a good practice to set up all of the available apparatus and allow the class to have a Free Play period. Such a procedure will help to dissolve any monotony that might have developed during a period of time as well as to give the students a free opportunity to express themselves. The teacher and his squad leaders during this period should carefully supervise the activities and be ready to discourage any "horse play" that might develop.

Table 1
RECOMMENDED TIME SPLITS FOR PROGRESSIVE GYMNASTICS

	45 min.	60 min.	90 min.
1. Dress for class	5	5	5
2. Roll call	1	1	2
3. Conditioning exercises	4	5	8
4. Explanation, demonstration and review	5	9	10
5. Practice of skill (including station change)	20	30	50
6. Showering and dressing	10	10	15

Squad Leaders in Group Participation

A properly administered "leader" training program can be instrumental in the success of progressive gymnastics. Since it is literally impossible for an instructor to be at two different stations at the same time, it is most advisable that teachers select a particular group of boys and train them to be squad leaders. This can be accomplished during club periods as well as after school.

These students should be chosen according to their leadership, performance of skill, character, and personality. By having them placed at each gymnastic station, they serve as reliable spotters and demonstrators. The class will unquestionably accept the squad leaders because they know these boys are there to assist them. The leaders can either rotate with their squads or remain at one particular station. This procedure will provide the student assistants with a sense of responsibility and a unique opportunity to develop their leadership abilities. This type of teaching situation enables the instructor to survey the class from a central point where he can see all that is progressing. In the event he feels that his direct assistance is required at a particular station, he merely has to remedy the situation and return to his station. If there is a particularly slow group in the class, he has the option of working directly with these boys.

It should be strongly pointed out to these leaders that they are not privileged characters and at no point should they treat the remaining group as plebes. Since "boys will be boys," a constant vigilance should be kept on their individual assistance. In this manner the situation will always be under the instructor's direct control.

Squad Formations for Teaching Gymnastics

A very important aspect of successful teaching is class organization. The different formations will vary according to the dimensions of the room to be used, the size of the squads and the particular segment of gymnastics being taught.

Small and Medium Sized Groups

The following information can be used for groups of less than 15 pupils.

Front line formation: The group forms a perpendicular line approximately 10 feet from the apparatus. This is the most common formation used when teaching apparatus and exhibitional gymnastics (*see* Diag. 1).

Cross line formation: The group forms a straight line behind the apparatus. This formation is commonly used in both Side and Long Horse Vaulting and Rope Climbing (*see* Diag. 2).

V- formation: The group forms a "V." The apparatus is placed in the center of the open end. This method can be used for almost any phase of gymnastics (*see* Diag. 3).

Semicircle formation: The group forms a semicircle with the apparatus in the center of the open end. This is also a very good formation for all gymnastic activity (*see* Diag. 4).

Parallel formation: The group forms two parallel lines with the apparatus placed in the center of the formation. A very good method for most gymnastic activity and especially useful in inter-squad competition (*see* Diag. 5).

Medium and Large Sized Groups

The following method formation can be used for groups of more than 15 pupils.

Mass formation: The group forms horizontal staggered lines behind the apparatus. A good formation for teaching by the class method and very beneficial in free calisthenics (*see* Diag. 6).

Multi-line formation: The group forms three parallel lines behind the apparatus. A very good formation for climbing when more than one rope is being used (*see* Diag. 7).

When using any of the previous formations, the students should be arranged to allow for freedom of movement and also so they can see and hear all that is taking place.

Lesson Plan

The primary purpose of lesson planning is to provide the instructor with a teaching guide to assist him in achieving the program's objectives. Program planning is usually divided into two major

Diags. 1-7: Formations Illustrated

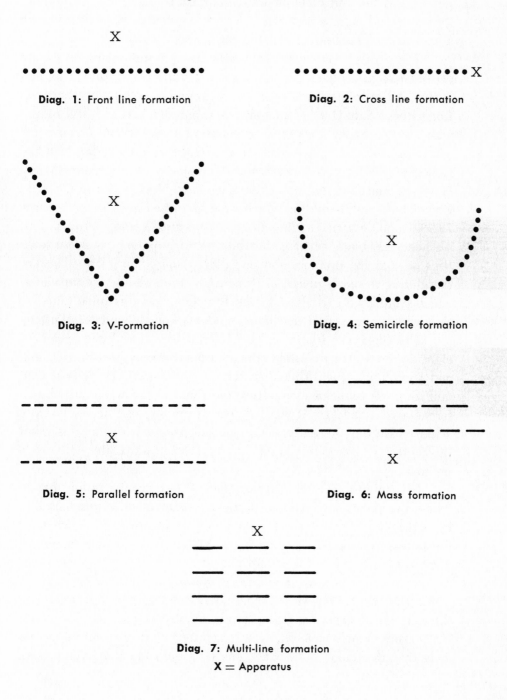

Diag. 1: Front line formation

Diag. 2: Cross line formation

Diag. 3: V-Formation

Diag. 4: Semicircle formation

Diag. 5: Parallel formation

Diag. 6: Mass formation

Diag. 7: Multi-line formation

X = Apparatus

categories: the daily lesson plan, or preparing for a particular class period; and the unit plan, or preparing for a segment of class periods. Due to its individualistic nature, progressive gymnastics calls for both administrative techniques to fulfill its goals.

The program is organized into six major unit plans. They are classified as BEGINNER, NOVICE, INTERMEDIATE, JUNIOR, ADVANCED, and SENIOR. All of the units contain the all-around events (Floor Exercise, Long Horse, Side Horse, Horizontal Bar, Parallel Bars and Still Rings) which are recognized by the Federation of International Gymnastics, The Amateur Athletic Union of the United States, The National Collegiate Athletic Association and the majority of scholastic leagues. However, the first two units, Beginner and Novice, (in addition to Rope Climb and Tumbling which were described in Chapter 5, pages 70-73) include a ninth division of gymnastics, namely Stunts. This segment, although outside the all-around program, was included because it is my opinion, and one that is shared by many teachers, that during the early phases of gymnastics stunts should be introduced which would tend to alleviate the formality and discipline allied to the gymnastic program that many students find difficult to adjust to.

The third and fourth units, (Intermediate and Junior) contain eight divisions of gymnastics (the all-around events plus Rope Climb and Tumbling). The fifth and sixth units (Advanced and Senior) contain seven divisions of gymnastics; the Rope Climb was omitted as a formal activity because it was felt that its purpose can be significantly achieved during the early phases of the program and at this point the students' energies should be directed toward the all-around program.

In arranging the daily lesson plan, the instructor simply has to follow the progression for the particular segment of gymnastics that he is teaching. Start with skill number one and proceed down until the unit is completed, keeping in mind that the program should be administered to allow for progression at all gymnastic stations. This procedure will develop all-around gymnastic competencies and discourage apparatus favoritism. The individual situation will determine the number of exercises to be taught at any given time. However, for maximum achievement, it is suggested that you introduce no more than three new skills at any one station during any given period.

Reviewing of Progress

When the class completes the divisional circuit and the individual squads start to repeat a particular station, always have them review all previous exercises that they attempted during the course of the semester before proceeding to the newly introduced skills. These can be practiced one at a time or, to economize, the instructor could plan a routine that would encompass the learned skills.

A suggested point value has been given to each exercise. This information will serve as an excellent basis for grading as well as to stimulate student participation. Totaled, these values equal 100%.

It is advisable to keep an accurate account of pupil progress on check sheets (Table 2). These records should be posted to keep students informed as to their personal progress and also to serve as a stimulus to help pupils strive for maximum potential. The progress sheets should also be kept on file to enable the instructor to determine the level at which the pupil progressed at the conclusion of each term. If a student does not satisfactorily complete all of the skills at any given station for a particular unit, he should be made to repeat those exercises during the ensuing term. Since each exercise serves as a basis for the following skill, it is absolutely essential that *each unit be chronologically completed.* A grade of 8.0 out of a possible 10 should be attained before a student receives credit for the skill.

Table 2

BEGINNER SKILLS

Point
Value

Free Calisthenics (14 pts.)

Point Value	Skill
2	1. five push-ups
2	2. tip up (3 seconds)
3	3. from a kick-up position hollow back roll to knee stand
1	4. front support
1	5. back support
2	6. scale (supporting leg in flexed position)
3	7. tuck, pike and layout position

Point
Value

Buck Vaulting (14 pts.)

   A. Buck in even position

2   1. flank vault
2   2. front vault
3   3. squat vault
2   4. straddle vault

   B. Buck in cross position

3   1. squat vault
2   2. straddle vault

Side Horse (6 pts.)

1   1. front support over saddle
1   2. rear support over saddle
2   3. flank vault over croup and neck
2   4. rear vault over croup and neck

Horizontal Bar (12 pts.)

2   1. three chins with reverse grip
2   2. three toe touches with regular grip
3   3. skin the cat
3   4. swing with good form
2   5. knee hang

Parallel Bars (15 pts.)

2   1. three dips
3   2. walk the length of the bars
3   3. cross straddle seats (3)
2   4. jump to lower arm support and swing
2   5. jump to upper arm support and swing
3   6. front dismount to cross side stand

Still Rings (13 pts.)

3   1. swing with good form
4   2. inverted hang in pike position

Point
Value

3   3. bird's nest hang
3   4. bent arm hang in pike position

Tumbling (9 pts.)
2   1. shoulder roll
2   2. forward roll
2   3. back roll
3   4. cartwheel

Rope Climb (8 pts.)
8   1. climb rope using feet (10 feet)

Stunts (9 pts.)
2   1. wheel barrow
2   2. monkey walks
2   3. three-man pyramids
3   4. log rolls

Pupil's Name _____

Class____ _____   Section _____

Year_____   Term_____

Additional Comments

    Additional student interest can be encouraged by having the pupils plan routines out of the learned skills. This process can eventually lead to competitive and exhibitional teams. When this objective is achieved, gymnastics will have made a definite stand in your total program.

    Invariably, we shall be dealing with a multitude of situations; therefore, individual programs should be made flexible enough to meet the different needs that may arise. At some point you will find students unable to learn a particular skill. Since we do not want to sacrifice mastery for variety, it would be wise to change the exercise or even the apparatus if the group is not properly adjusting to the lesson. On the other hand, if a particular squad accomplishes the lesson with ease, they should be given every opportunity to progress further. In either case, the instructor should not rush students through the program in order to meet a preplanned deadline. This procedure will only defeat the program's objectives.

Time is an essential factor in fulfilling the program's objectives. Gymnastics skills have their best application to a student's motor development when applied on a continuous six-to-eight-week unit plan. Curriculum planning of this nature will provide the instructor with the necessary time so essential for successful completion of the individual units. Thus, teaching will be more meaningful to the entire situation and the program's objectives will be accomplished.

Safety

Suggestions

III

Knowledge of safety techniques in gymnastic activity is a very important teaching prerequisite. The instructor should be aware of all available safeguards and should be able to forsee when their application will be necessary. Strict adherence to this principle must be applied from the simple forward roll in tumbling to the difficult German giant swing on the horizontal bar.

Due to the possible severity of any injury that might be incurred while learning gymnastics, we cannot permit any margin of error. Therefore, when we speak of "Safety Suggestions," the entire apparatus program is taken into account. In an effort to prevent safety "loopholes" in progressive gymnastics, this chapter will deal wtih the following three aspects of the training program:

1. Pre-workout period
2. Workout period
3. Post-workout period

Pre-Workout Period

The pre-workout period includes all of those activities and procedures that prepare the individual for the actual instruction and practice of gymnastic skills.

Conditioning and Warm-up

The gymnastics instructor will find many of his students lacking in general motor ability or the ability to perform, as the apparatus program commences. These deficiences will eventually be subdued through participation in gymnastic activity. However, one should not rely on this if optimum safety is to prevail.

A conditioning program aimed at alleviating pupil's fitness deficiences should be administered in the physical education program prior to starting of apparatus activity. Such a developmental program will serve as a prerequisite for the desired state of body tonus which is of utmost importance for the safe execution of gymnastic exercises.

A weight training program of gradually increasing severity is a very good conditioning activity. Such resistive exercising three days per week is sufficient training. If such a conditioning program cannot be made possible, any activity that stresses the development of physical fitness qualities, with emphasis on strength, should be employed.

At the beginning of each class period a thorough warm-up of at least five minutes should be given to the entire group. This phase of the exercise program is vitally needed to alert and prepare the entire body for immediate strenuous activity, which might otherwise cause serious harm to the muscular system. A calisthenics drill in which there is progression in the speed of the exercise and degree of exertion will prove to be helpful before the starting of the class period. Special attention should be given to the limbering of the muscles in the neck, shoulders, arms, back, abdomen, lateral trunk and legs.

The following series of movements will prove to be very beneficial prior to participation in apparatus exercises:

1. Neck Rotation:

From a regular stand with feet shoulder width apart, place hands on hips and slowly rotate neck clockwise and then repeat counter-clockwise (*see Diag. 8*).

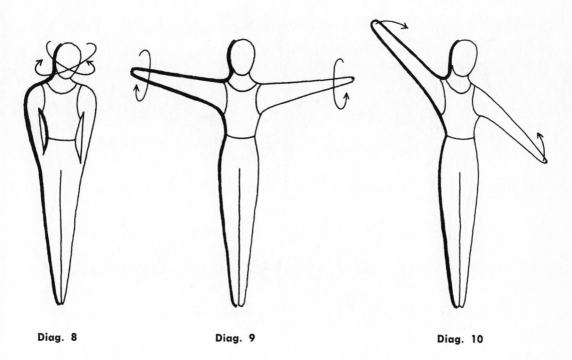

Diag. 8   **Diag. 9**   **Diag. 10**

2. Arm Circumduction:

From a regular stand with feet shoulder width apart, stretch arms sideways; rotate arms forward and then back (*Diag. 9*).

3. Diagonal Stretch:

From a regular stand with feet shoulder width apart, place arms in a diagonal position. Stretch arms back by emphasizing pull from the shoulders. Repeat by switching the arm position (*Diag. 10*).

4. Oblique Bends:

From a regular stand with feet shoulder width apart, place hands on hips and slowly lower body to right side and then return to original position and repeat to the left side (*Diag. 11*).

5. Anthero Posteria's:

From a regular stand with feet shoulder width apart, bend forward with straight knees and touch floor; return to standing position and then lean back into arched position. Return to stand and repeat. Emphasize upward tilt of the pelvic girdle while in the posterior position (*Diag. 12*).

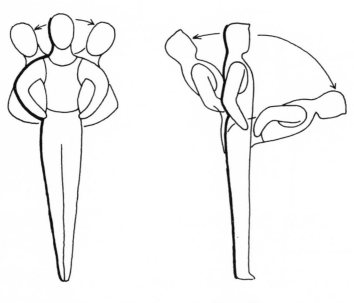

Diag. 11   Diag. 12   Diag. 13

6. Squats:

From a regular stand with feet shoulder width apart, place hands on hips. Slowly squat down while on toes and return to stand. Care should be given to maintain the torso in an upright position. Many students tend to overflex the hips and cause the trunk to lean forward. Return to stand and repeat (*Diag. 13*).

7. Elevators:

From a regular stand with feet shoulder-width apart, place hands and arms in an extended position, on the back of a chair or on a partner's shoulders. With the head in an upright position force the shoulders down and brace the body with straight legs. Maintain the position and continue the contraction (*Diags. 14, 14-a*).

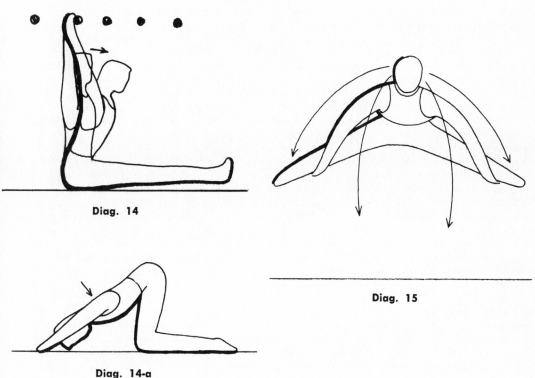

Diag. 14

Diag. 15

Diag. 14-a

8. Straddle Leans:

From a sitting position with legs in straddle position, lean to the right side and flex the hips as much as possible without bending the knee. Repeat on other side (*Diag. 15*).

9. Sit-ups:

From a sitting position with hands behind neck and knees in full flexion, lie back until the back is parallel to the floor and then return to the starting position. If it is found too difficult to exercise the

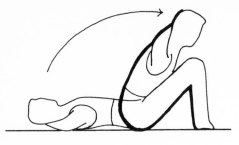

Diag. 16

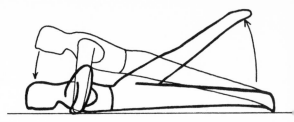

Diag. 17

maneuver with the knee in full flexion, slowly extend the knee until the sit-up can be performed. Full flexion of the knee is most beneficial for exercising the abdominal wall (*Diag. 16*).

10. Hyper-extended Push-ups:

From a front support position, lower the body to the floor by flexing the elbow; at the same time hyper-extend the right leg. Return to starting position and continue push-ups, alternating the hyper-extension of both legs (*Diag. 17*).

Apparatus and Mats

At the beginning of each class period or practice session the apparatus and mats should be thoroughly inspected to insure that they are in proper working condition and satisfactorily set up.

The immediate surrounding area about each piece of apparatus must be covered with a sufficient number of mats if optimum safety is to prevail. Their main function is to protect the student against accidental falls to the floor as well as to absorb the shock and cushion all landings when decending from various heights. Mats also aid the students psychologically by helping to create a feeling of sureness while mastering the various skills.

1. Hair and Felt Type Mats: The following pad sizes are recommended for gymnastic activity when utilizing the hair and felt type mats:

Free Exercise:	Tie mats together to form a 40′ x 40′ area. It is advisable to put large mats on the outer borders to help hold the regular mats in place. (*Diag. 18*)
Long Horse:	one 5′ x 20′ or two 5′ x 10′ covered with an

additional two 5′ x 10′ (at the neck end); two 5′ x 7′ (at even sides).

Buck:	two 5′ x 10′ covered with an additional 5′ x 10′ at the neck end
Side Horse:	four 5′ x 7′ or two 5′ x 10′
Horizontal Bar:	one 5′ x 20′ covered with a 5′ x 10′ on either side of the bar
Parallel Bars:	two 5′ x 10′ (at even sides); two 5′ x 7′ (on ends); one 3′ x 7′ (in middle).
Still Rings:	one 5′ x 10′
Tumbling:	one 6′ x 50′ or two 5′ x 20′
Ropes:	one 5′ x 10′ (for each rope)

Diag. 18: Formulating a floor exercise area, 12 by 12 meters, from 32 hair felt mats, 5 by 10 ft. each.

Pyramids: Mat sizes will vary according to the number of
                             pupils involved in the pyramid. However, a
                             minimum 5′ x 10′ mat should always be used
                             for this activity.

Stunts: three 5′ x 10′ or one 5′ x 20′

(All hair–felt type of mats should be a minimum of 2″ thick.)

2. **Plastic Foam Type Mats:** The advent of the plastic foam type of
mat (also referred to as cellular plastic foam and *Rubatex*) has given
new dimensions to safety and convenience in apparatus activities. This
rubber base allows for lightness in handling and absorbancy upon
landing. The mats are one inch in thickness and this compactness has
been claimed to equal four inches of the hair–felt type mats.

The various sizes can be custom cut or they can be basically the
same size as the hair–felt mats. However, their lightness and storage
accessibility enables all situations to utilize the 5′ x 20′, 5′ x 30′ and even
the 5′ x 40′ sizes. The one-inch thickness will suffice for most stations;
however, you should double up the pads in areas where the adjoining
mats are apt to separate when landed upon, such as in long horse
vaulting and in tumbling.

In Figures 1-5, the placement of the plastic foam mats when used
with the basic gymnastic equipment is illustrated.

Fig. 1: The Side Horse   Fig. 2: The Long Horse

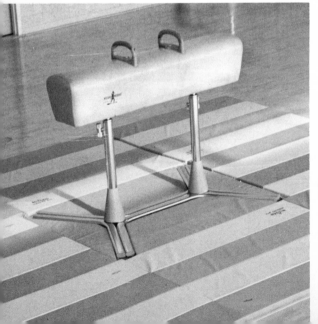

Fig. 3: The Horizontal Bar

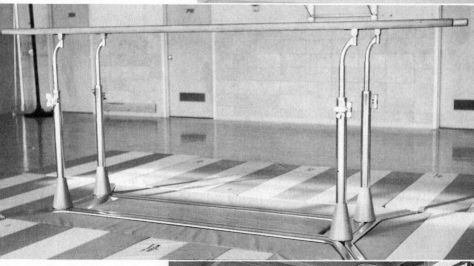

Fig. 4: The Parallel Bars

Fig. 5: The Still Rings

Fig. 6-a

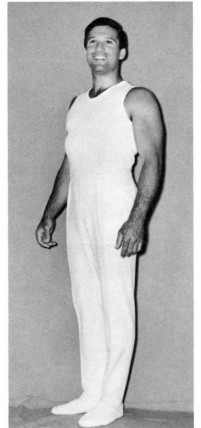

Fig. 6-b

Fig. 6-c

Uniforms

The uniform for gymnastic activity (*See Fig. 6, a* through *c*) should consist of a tee shirt, athletic supporter, shorts, sweat socks, and pumps. It is not advisable to wear loose clothing such as a sweat suit during the actual performance; the extra material often hinders a good exercise plus the fact that it covers up the student's true form. A pair of snug fitting trousers may be substituted for the shorts and in cases where the upper arms have become tender, such as from upper arm supports on the parallel bars, a tight-fitting long-sleeved garment should be worn for future protection.

Supervision

In spite of repeated warnings, you will always find a select group of pupils hurrying to the gymnasium to engage in pre-class "fooling around." It is therefore advisable to have someone supervising at all times and in turn try to encourage these early arrivals to engage in constructive exercises. This procedure will increase skill interest and reduce mishaps.

Workout Period

The workout period includes all of those activities and procedures that enable the individual to safely engage in the actual practice of gymnastic skills.

Safety Instruction

Safety instruction should be incorporated into every gymnastics lesson plan. This phase of apparatus training is so important to the success of a program that it cannot be overemphasized. During the demonstrations and reviews of skills, classes should be made aware of the necessary precautions for maximum safety during the course of any one exercise or routine.

General Safety Suggestions for the Performer

1. Pay strict attention to the description and demonstration of each new exercise.
2. Ask questions when in doubt.

3. Be sure to have a spotter on hand before attempting an exercise.
4. Use plenty of magnesium carbonate when needed.
5. Master the fundamentals.
6. Do not try stunts beyond your level of difficulty or until the instructor has "checked" you out.
7. Come to a stop when the whistle is blown.
8. Do not act foolishly during classes.
9. If a slip occurs during your performance, try to relax, give with the fall and follow with a roll if and when possible.

Spotting

The art of spotting or safeguarding the individual is probably the most important safety element in all gymnastics. The feeling of sureness and trust in one's fellow man that results from such a program is second only to individual success.

Accidents that occur in apparatus and tumbling training never "just happen." They are caused. Because of this truth one must prepare himself and his assistants for any mishap that might result from practicing the exercises. Pushing, holding, lifting, catching or adjusting the performer are all spotting essentials that are required to prevent injurious falls. Each of the exercises in progressive gymnastics can be assisted by one or more of the previous spotting elements.

General Spotting Suggestions for the Instructor

1. Before assigning leaders to the various gymnastic stations, they should be thoroughly instructed as to the difficulty, execution and proper safeguards of every move that they will be assisting.
2. Maintain a constant safety attitude during class. It can be very contagious.
3. Spotters should have a "clear picture" of what the performer is about to try and the delicate points that need precise attention during its execution.
4. No matter what the ability of the student may be, never "sell him short" by relaxing and taking his performance for granted. One never knows when a mishap may occur.
5. Do not over-spot a performer to the point where he will

constantly depend on your direct assistance for skill execution; thus, he will not have obtained a feeling of self-confidence that is very much desired in gymnastics.

6. Always have your strong arm in ready position for a possible mishap. There is a right and a wrong side for every stunt.
7. Learn to recognize unsureness of the performer. This can be seen in the forms of fearful attitudes, facial expressions and his general execution of skill.
8. If a fleeting body has lost control in space, try to spot the man from his neck or back by planting him on his feet, knees or even in a prone position. These positions are less harmful than having the man land on his head, neck or back.

Specific Spotting Suggestions for the Instructor

Floor Exercise: Whenever a performer tries a handstand, make certain that he knows how to twist or roll out in case of an overbalance. In the early stages of learning, controlling the performer by supporting the boy's legs proves to be very beneficial. This technique also applies to the headstand.

In the early stages of learning the back roll, the instructor can alleviate unnecessary neck strain by supporting the performer's neck with either hand.

The cartwheel action can be supplemented by holding the student's hips from his rear, once he starts into the handstand position and by guiding him through the handstand and back onto his feet.

Backbend movements should be supported by controlling the lower back to prevent possible back strain. Before attempting any excessive stretching maneuvers, such as the split, have the student thoroughly warm up that particular region of the body.

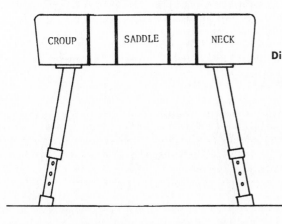

CROUP SADDLE NECK

Diag. 19: Positions of the horse. On the side horse, the croup is to the right of the performer, while the neck is to his left. On the long horse, the neck is the farthest position from the inclined board while the croup is the nearest position to the inclined board.

Long Horse in the Even Position: In spotting the front and flank vaults, stand to the opposite side of where the performer's legs are passing over the apparatus; hold his near arm and wrist firmly and guide him through the maneuver. A straddle vault spot requires that you stand facing the student (the spotter should be cautious not to stand too close to the performer as this stance will only stymie his performance) and spot by stabilizing the student's upper arms or chest. The squat vault calls for a side spot. Control the student by grasping his arm.

Long Horse in the Cross Position: In long horse vaulting, a spotter should always be ready for a student to over-spin or over-rotate a jump. A good rule to follow is to watch the performer's chest and be ready to move in to support if and when necessary.

Side Horse: In spotting dismounts where the body passes over the front cross rest position, as in the loop off, wait until the student's legs pass you and then move in with a rear hip spot.

Whenever a vault, which involves a half turn in execution, is used, spot the wrist and forearm and continue to spot until the student has positively completed the half turn.

In executing the double leg circle, the student sometimes tends to lean too far back in an effort to maintain his balance. This should be carefully watched by standing to the rear of the performer and being alert to support him in the event he should fall backward.

Horizontal Bar: In any turning motion around the transverse axis, while in the hanging position, as in the skin-the-cat, spot the student from the upper back; as the turn nears completion move in and offer support to his chest with one hand and to his neck with the other. Thus, if he falls down or over-spins, you will have complete control of his body.

Whenever a student is in a knee hang, make certain that his feet are dorsiflexed; this will insure a firmer knee grip.

Always keep a watchful eye on a student's hand grip while he is swinging on the bar. Often you can detect a student's slipping by the position of his original grip; this situation should receive your immediate attention.

Any dismount which involves the performer passing under the bar without entailing a full circular motion, as in the short underswing, spot by keeping your ready arm in position to support the student's back in the event he does not complete his rotation.

In circling around the bar, from a hanging position, always make certain that the student assumes a regular grip for backward movements and a reverse grip for forward movements. In the event that you discover an improper grip, be prepared to stop the student by grabbing him around the waist as quickly as possible.

When the student attempts the three-quarter back giant swing, follow him around very closely giving special consideration to his upper back. In the event of a slip, control him by keeping one hand on his back until he is safely returned to the floor.

Stay close to a student when the cast half turn is attempted. Often the outside hand fails to regrip the bar; this situation requires a waist spot until the boy can regain his grip.

Dismounts coming down from over the bar, as the sole circle dismount, require the spotter to stand in a rear oblique position in relation to the student. As he is executing the skill move out with him, paying strict attention to his upper back. For over-rotation, move in and spot by placing your hand on his upper back; for under rotation, move in and spot by placing your hand on his chest.

All giant swings should be spotted directly beneath the bar. In the event the student misses the trick and starts to descend the wrong way, move in and stop his rotation before he passes the mid-point by grabbing his upper legs with your arms.

Parallel Bars: Whenever a student is walking or swinging from a lower arm support, keep a watchful eye that he does not uncontrollably fall forward and hyper-extend the shoulder region. This can be checked by preventing the performer's legs from going astray (as in the walk from the lower arm support) by controlling them with your hands. Falling forward in the swing can be spotted by supporting the performer's chest.

Never spot a swinging body passing from above to below the bars with your hand or arm between the student and the bars as in reaching over the bar to spot an over-balanced hand or shoulder stand. This can only lead to serious injury on the part of the spotter.

Cut mounts from the cross position should be spotted from the student's rear either by holding his trousers top or by supporting his back as he passes through the maneuver.

Whenever a student attempts a half turn from a support position, always instruct him to keep one hand or arm intact until he can clearly observe the new position; this will prevent lower body scrapes.

In spotting a backward or forward roll, always be cautious that the student does not release his grip too soon thus causing him to slide out of control and possibly fall off the bars. In the event this occurs, spot the student's back from beneath the bars.

For spotting vault mounts and dismounts, *see* Long Horse.

Mounts, from the middle of the bars should be spotted beneath the bars by continuously supporting the student's chest or back (according to the exercise he is attempting).

Rings: Whenever a student does a circular or turning motion beneath the rings, as in the skin-the-cat, stabilize his body and assist by placing one hand on his upper back. As the turn passes the mid-point, transfer your assistance to his chest, keeping your free arm in readiness, should he over-rotate and fall off balance. These two spotting techniques will keep the spotter in control of the student, if he should suddenly lose his grip.

During the early stages of practicing the lower arm support, be ready to grab the student's legs if he should suddenly lose control.

In spotting dismounts on the rings, stand about one foot behind the mid-point and place yourself in a rear oblique position in relation to the student. When the dismount is attempted, particular consideration should be given to over-rotation on backward dismounts and to under-rotation on forward dismounts. These occurrences should be spotted by moving in, either on the chest (to keep the anterior portion of the body from striking the floor) or the upper back and neck (to keep the posterior portion of the body from striking the floor).

Inlocates should be spotted by moving your strong hand onto the boy's chest immediately after he passes the mid-point; as soon as the body inlocates, give support to the upper back.

Whenever a student attempts to pass from a lower arm support to a hang, whether he goes straight through or rolls forward or back, spot the movement by supporting the upper back. Often the sudden drop puts an enormous strain on the shoulders and this could possibly cause the student to lose his grip.

Spot dislocates by first lifting the student's chest and with the left hand and then supporting his back, with the right hand. This will give support to sudden strains that usually accompany the learning of this maneuver.

Backward turning movements going from beneath to above the rings as in the back kip, should be carefully spotted by controlling the student's legs, should he miss the lower arm support and fall through to a hanging position.

Tumbling: Dive forward rolls should be spotted by carefully watching the position of the student's back. In the event of an over-rotation, move in and give support to the upper back.

The hand spring should be spotted by placing your hand on the student's upper back as he goes into the handstand position; stay with him to insure a safe landing. The head spring is spotted in a similar manner.

In spotting the back hand spring, move onto the student's lower back as he loses his balance; continue to give support until the turn is completed.

The back somersault should be spotted by placing your hand on the performer's back as he attempts the stunt; continue giving support until the student makes a half turn; at this point move in behind his neck to safeguard against over-rotation.

Spot the front flip by placing your hand behind the student's neck as he attempts the stunt; stay with him until completion.

Supervision

During the workout period, the instructor should assume a direct supervisory role over the total situation. You should be in such a position as to view the class as a whole. The best way to accomplish this technique is to have the individual squads under the indirect control of capable leaders. While they are assisting the individual groups, you will be able to contribute to the situation a personal maximum coverage which in turn will provide you with a teaching freedom. This makes your teaching more effective and purposeful.

During this period, it is adamantly recommended that you *never* leave the teaching situation unless a co-worker substitutes for your position. As effective as your leaders may be, they are still students and are not physically, mentally or emotionally capable of assuming your role in the capacity of instructor of physical education.

Post-Workout Period

The post-workout period includes all of those practices that help to maintain adequate procedures necessary for the well-being of the individual.

Securing Equipment

Whenever the gymnastics program is not in operation, the gymnasium should be free of all hazardous conditions. The last gymnastics class out should secure the apparatus in the following manner:

1. Secure all suspended equipment such as rings and ropes.
2. Secure apparatus and mats in their proper locations.
3. Lock springboards, trampolettes and trampolines.
4. When storing for an extended period of time, a thin coat of vaseline will protect the horizontal bar from rust.
5. Remove all excessive chalk that might accumulate on the gymnasium floor.
6. Lock the gymnasium.

In the event the gymnasium is left open for an incoming class, a teacher should be on hand to supervise at all times.

Proper Care of the Body

Students should be urged to report all injuries to the instructor as soon as they occur. In this manner, strained muscle fibers, sprained ligaments, and "torn hands" can be checked and remedied with minimum delay. In caring for the hands, the use of tincture of benzoin on relatively soft palms will help to harden the skin for apparatus use, while a petroleum jelly will prevent the hands from cracking and peeling once a callus has been attained. It is also advisable to have the student stretch out at the conclusion of a workout. This is an excellent practice to keep the body limber.

During the course of the instructional period, the student's hands might very likely become so tender that a preventive taping of the affected area would be advisable. Similarly, the wrists, due to the constant support and hanging, would also require a preventive taping. However, it should be noted that in severe cases a physician should be consulted.

Taping the Hand and Wrist for Apparatus Use

A. Taping the palm
   1. Shave excess hair from the wrist and lower portion of the

forearm. Spray the hand (front and back) and wrist with tincture of benzoin to increase the cohesiveness of the tape (*Fig. 7*).

2. Apply a 1″ strip of tape around the lower forearm approximately 2½″ up from the wrist. With the hand in prone position, anchor a ¾″ strip to the circular base strip; with the hand in full extension, carry the strip between the little finger and its adjoining finger, supinate the hand, carry the strip over the palm and anchor to the circular base strip (*Fig. 7*).

3. Apply ¾″ strips between the second and third, and the third and fourth fingers (*Fig. 8*).

4. Anchor the ends of the strips with a 1″ strip around the lower forearm (*Fig. 9*).

Figs. 7-12: Taping the palm

Fig. 7

Fig. 8

Fig. 9

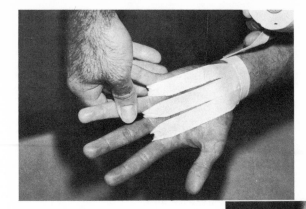

Fig. 10

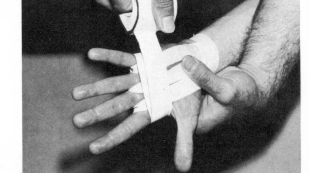

Fig. 11

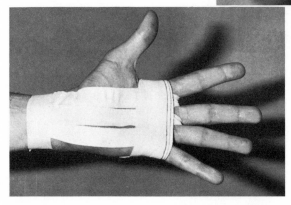

Fig. 12

5. Apply a 1½″ strip over the medial portion of the center knuckle, and carry the strip around to the palm, placing the tape at the base of the fingers; continue the strip around the hand and anchor at the point of origin. It should be emphasized that the hand should remain in extension throughout the entire taping (*Figs. 10-12*).

B. Taping the wrist*
    1. Shave excessive hair off the lower arm and wrist. With
       the hand in *full extension* apply a 1″ strip around the base
       of the wrist. Tape from lateral to medial or from thumb
       to little finger (*Fig. 13*).
    2. Apply a second strip of 1″ tape approximately ½″ behind
       the base strip (*Fig. 14*).

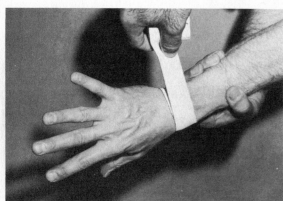

Figs. 13-15: Taping the wrist

Fig. 13

Fig. 14

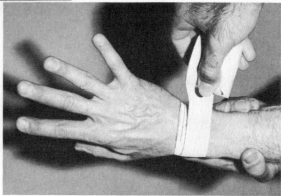

    3. Finish the wrap with two 1½″ strips, approximately ¼″
       behind the base strip (*Fig. 15*).

---

* The tension of the individual strips, when taping the wrists, should be snug but
not tight enough to interfere with circulation, which might cause the tips of the fingers
to change color.

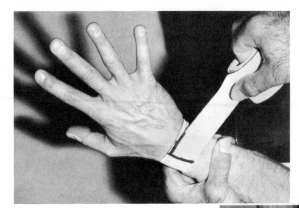

Fig. 15

Fig. 16

4. Note a complete job of wrist and hand taping, showing placement of palm guards as a final protection against friction (*Fig. 16*).

Gymnastic

Nomenclature

and Basic Body Positions

IV

The diversification of body positions and movements in gymnastics makes it necessary to formulate a common language (nomenclature). Throughout the years, several systems have been devised. As applicable as they might be, there still exists a bewilderment among teachers, coaches, and students, especially among the beginners in these groups. Too often, various stunts are named after different gymnasts or given a sobriquet derived from a particular group. What is needed is a standard set of terms which can be used by teachers of gymnastics at all levels.

Progressive gymnastics, in employing its system of technical terms, has attempted to reduce the confusion which often accompanies the interpreting of the different exercises and combinations. It has condensed the complex terminology into simple, concise definitions, with accompanying diagrams, to increase understanding. It is strongly advised that the reader become thoroughly familiar with the nomenclature in this book. This will make skill interpretation more meaningful and exact to both teacher and student.

Basic Positions

The four basic positions employed in progressive gymnastics are: *Hangs, Stands, Supports,* and *Seats.* Whenever one assumes one of these basic positions he is either Cross or Even relative to the apparatus or floor. The term CROSS refers the position when the transverse axis of the body (picture a line *across* the chest) is perpendicular to the apparatus. The term EVEN applies when the transverse axis is parallel to the apparatus.

A Cross or Even relationship can occur in one of three ways: Rear Way, when one's back is toward the apparatus or floor; Front Way, when one's front is toward the apparatus or floor; Side Way, when one's side is toward the apparatus or floor (the side way position can be either left or right).

We have the following patterns that can be achieved:

	STANDS	
CROSS	SEATS	EVEN
(front, rear or side)	SUPPORTS	(front, rear or side)
	HANGS	

A typical example of the above application would be:

Cross right side stand
Even front support
Cross upper arm hang
Cross straddle seat

Stands, supports and seats are positions that can take place on the floor as well as on the apparatus, while the hang position can take place only on the apparatus.

Cross and Even Stands

(*Diags. 20, 21, 22, 27, 28, 29, 30, 46, 47, 48, 49, 50, 51*)

Stands are usually classified as *Straight Stands* (the majority of the weight being on the feet) and *Inverted Stands* (the majority of the weight being on the hands, head, etc.). On the parallel bars, the Cross Stands at the near and far ends are distinguished from the Cross Stand Front Ways and Rear Ways in that the former stands are performed *outside* of the bars.

Cross and Even Seats

(*Diags. 24, 55, 56*)

In assuming a *seat* position, the majority of the weight is centered on the buttocks or upper legs. On the parallel bars the cross seats may be classified as inner and outer seats while cross straddle seats are often called cross riding seats.

Cross and Even Supports

(*Diags. 23, 24, 25, 26, 31, 32, 39, 42, 44, 54, 59*)

In a *support* position the majority of the weight is born by the arms. Often, the arch position will force the thighs to come in contact with the apparatus, thus lessening the strain on the arms.

Cross and Even Hangs

(*Diags. 33, 34, 35, 36, 37, 38, 40, 41, 43, 45, 52, 53, 57, 58, 60*)

In the *hang* position the majority of weight is born by the hands or often by other parts of the body such as in the upper arm hang (upper arms) and the knee hang (the knees).

Mounts and Dismounts

A *mount* or a *start* is a maneuver which commences a given exercise. It is usually executed from a standing position (except in the case of the rings and horizontal bar where mounts are started from a hanging position) and terminates, in most cases, in a hang or a support position (*Diag. 125*).

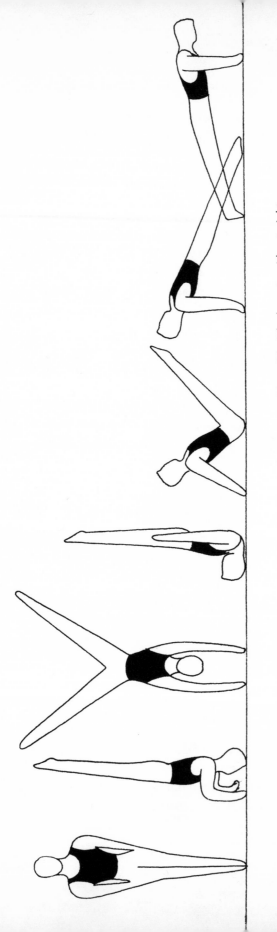

(left to right)

Diag. 20: Straight stand (on floor)

Diag. 21: Headstand (on floor)

Diag. 22: Hand or inverted stand, legs straddled (on floor)

Diag. 23: Shoulder support, body extended (on floor)

Diag. 24: Piked seat with straight arm support (on floor)

Diag. 25: Rear arched support (on floor)

Diag. 26: Front arched support (on floor)

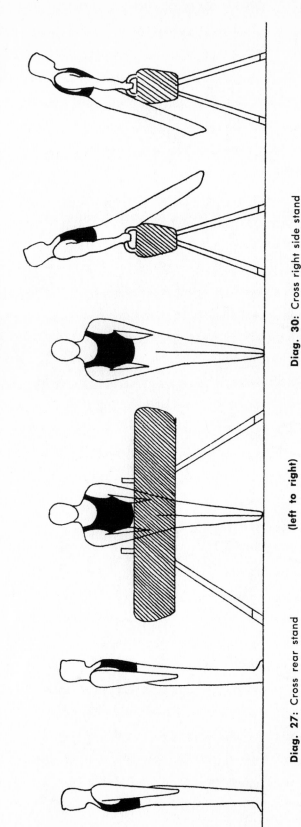

Diag. 27: Cross rear stand   (left to right)

Diag. 28: Cross front stand

Diag. 29: Even front stand

Diag. 30: Cross right side stand

Diag. 31: Even rear support

Diag. 32: Even front support

49

Diag. 33: Even hang with regular grip or over-grasp

Diag. 34: Even hang with reverse grip or under-grasp

Diag. 35: Even hang with crossed over-grasp

(left to right)

Diag. 36: Even hang with combined grip (right over, left under)

Diag. 37: Even hang with crossed combined grip (right over, left under)

Diag. 38: Even hang with rotated grasp (outward)

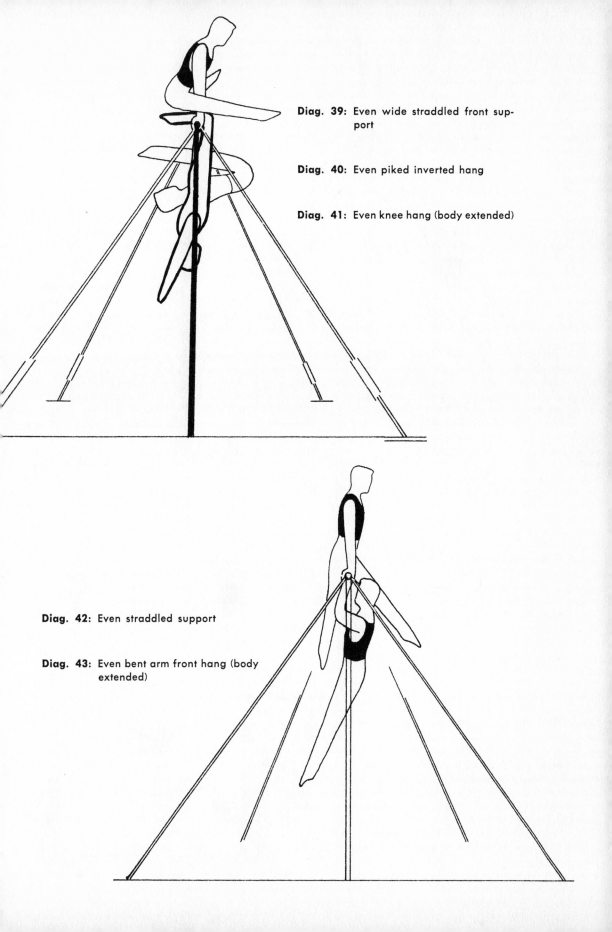

Diag. 39: Even wide straddled front support

Diag. 40: Even piked inverted hang

Diag. 41: Even knee hang (body extended)

Diag. 42: Even straddled support

Diag. 43: Even bent arm front hang (body extended)

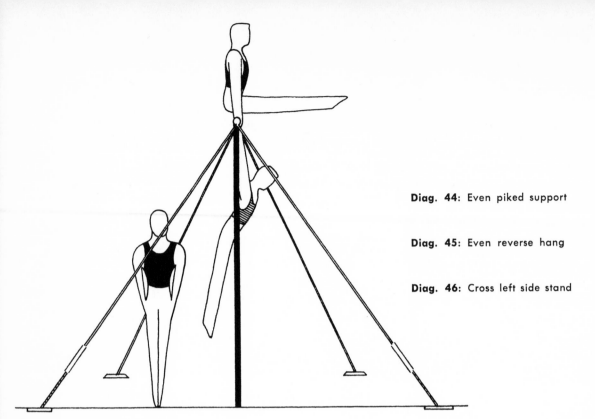

Diag. 44: Even piked support

Diag. 45: Even reverse hang

Diag. 46: Cross left side stand

Diag. 47: Cross rear stand or cross stand at far end

Diag. 48: Even handstand on one bar

Diag. 49: Even rear stand or even rear stand at far bar

Diag. 50: Cross handstand (on two bars)

Diag. 51: Cross front stand or cross stand at near end

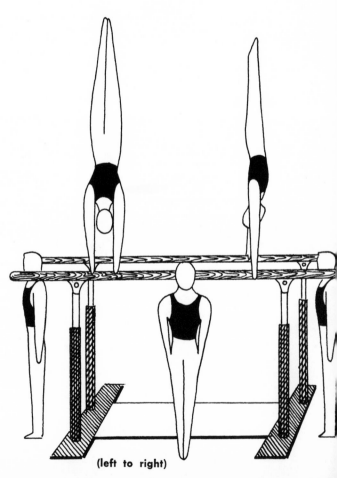

(left to right)

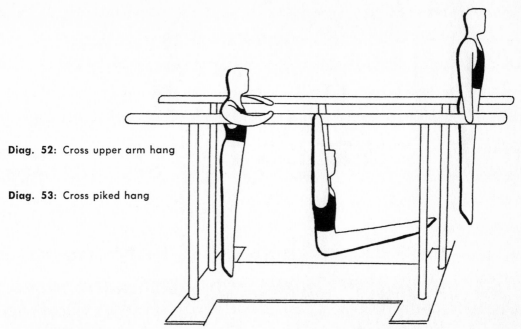

Diag. 52: Cross upper arm hang

Diag. 53: Cross piked hang

Diag. 54: Cross lower arm support or cross lower arm support at far end

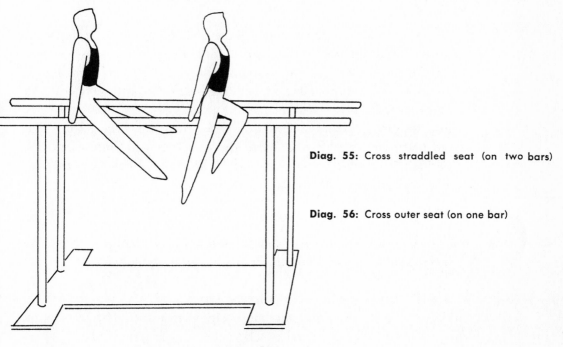

Diag. 55: Cross straddled seat (on two bars)

Diag. 56: Cross outer seat (on one bar)

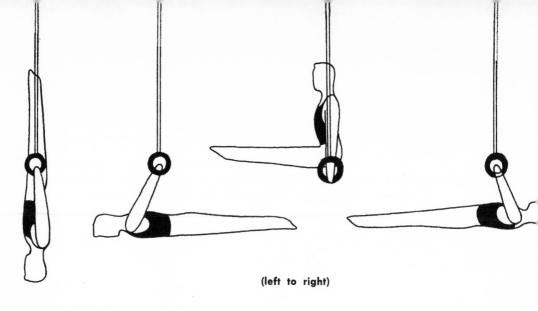

(left to right)

Diag. 57: Even straight body inverted hang

Diag. 58: Even back horizontal hang

Diag. 59: Even piked support

Diag. 60: Even front horizontal hang

A *dismount*, or a *finish*, is a maneuver which concludes a given exercise. It is executed from stands, hangs and supports and terminates in a straight stand on the floor (*Diag. 133*).

Vaults

A *vault* is a maneuver in which the body passes over the apparatus to a straight stand on the floor. In vaulting over the long horse or buck (in both the cross and even positions) the performer, after making his approach to the horse, takes off from the beat board with both feet and jumps over the horse with the hands momentarily supporting the body to a straight stand on the floor. Contrarily, there are certain vaults that are performed on the side horse that are executed from a starting position of support (as the rear and flank vaults) which serve as valuable dismounts for elementary routines.

Turns

A *turn* is a change of the body position by a rotating motion. The body revolves or pivots on the transverse or longitudinal axis.

1. TURNS FROM THE STANDING POSITION
   Most turns in a standing position have their line of rotation on the longitudinal axis. However, in a dive forward roll, which

54

is executed from the standing position, the pivot line is the transverse axis. All turns from the handstand position are generally referred to as *piorettes* (*Diags. 175-222*).

2. TURNS FROM THE HANGING POSITION

   Most hanging turns with the exception of knee turns are executed around the longitudinal axis (*Diag. 264*).

3. TURNS FROM THE SUPPORTIVE POSITION

   Turns from the supportive position utilize rotation on both the transverse and longitudinal axes. A three-quarters forward hip turn on the horizontal bar would be one example of rotation around the transverse axis while a dip one-half turn on the parallel bars would be rotation around the longitudinal axis (*Diags. 126-245*).

4. TURNS FROM THE SITTING POSITION

   Turns from the sitting position employ both longitudinal and transverse axes of rotation. A forward seat turn on the horizontal bar would utilize the transverse axis while a seat spin on the floor would utilize the longitudional axis (*Diag. 269*).

Feints

Any purposeful momentary pause in a turn to gather increased momentum in the opposite direction is referred to as a *feint*. This maneuver is usually performed on the side horse in learning the various Junior, Advanced and Senior skills (*Diag. 121*).

Twists

Twists are categorized as turns; however, in gymnastics these movements are classified as separate entities.

Circles

In order to perform a *circle*, an arc of 360° must be maintained. If the movement is not a complete circle it is called a turn. Circles can be initiated from the hanging, standing and supporting positions (*Diag. 163*).

Swings

A pendulum *swing* of the body is usually in a forward and backward motion. These movements vary in degree and occur in the hanging and supportive positions. In the hanging position the pivot line is the shoulders. On the side horse if one were to swing his body, it would be from side to side rather than to and fro (*Diag. 124-262*).

Travels

A *travel* is the term designated for any movement by the gymnast where he moves from one zone or area to another without performing a turn with respect to his body position (*Diag. 119*).

Beginner

Skills

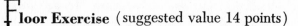

V

Floor Exercise (suggested value 14 points)

1. *Five Push-ups* (2 points) (*Diag. 61*)
   a. Assume a front support position as illustrated.
   b. Bend arms until abdomen and chest are within a few inches of the floor then return to starting position.

SPOTTING SUGGESTIONS

The instructor may place his hand under the student's mid-section to insure proper technique. Emphasize the maintaining of a straight back.

2. *Tip-up* (2 points) (*Diag. 62*)
   a. Assume a squat position with both hands flat on the floor, fingers facing forward and knees on the outside of the elbows.
   b. Brace the knees against the elbows and lean forward until a balanced position is assumed. Hold this position for three seconds. Return to the starting position.

SPOTTING SUGGESTIONS

The instructor may assist the student by holding his hips in a balanced position. Be sure to place a mat beneath the pupil's upper body. Often the lack of arm strength and balance will cause the performer to fall forward.

3. *Hollow Back Roll* (3 points) (*Diag. 63*)
   a. Kick to a three-quarter handstand position, as illustrated.
   b. Bring both legs together, bend both arms and lower the chest to the floor with an arched back position.
   c. As the thighs make contact with the floor, push vigorously with the hands and continue arching backwards until the full body weight is balanced on the feet and knees.

SPOTTING SUGGESTIONS

This movement should be practiced on a mat. The instructor may help by holding the student's feet in the three-quarter handstand position and lowering him into the chest roll.

4. *Front Support* (1 point) (*Diag. 64*)
   a. Assume the position, as illustrated, emphasizing the arched back position.
5. *Back Support* (1 point) (*Diag. 65*
   a. Assume the position, as illustrated, emphasizing the extended neck position.
6. *Bent Leg Scale* (2 points) (*Diag. 66*)
   a. Get down on hands and knees.

Diag. 61   Diag. 62   Diag. 63

Diag. 64   Diag. 65   Diag. 66

    b. Remove either arm and corresponding leg from the floor and stretch them, as illustrated. Hold this position without moving for three seconds.

SPOTTING SUGGESTIONS

    The instructor may adjust the student's limbs to insure the correct positions.

    7. *Tuck, Pike and Layout Positions* (3 points) (*Diag. 67*)

        a. Roll on the back several times, as illustrated.

        b. Hold the pike position, as illustrated, for three seconds.

        c. Hold the layout position, as illustrated, for three seconds.

Diag. 67

Buck Vaulting (suggested value 14 points)

A. Buck in Even Position

    1. *Flank Vault* (2 points) (*Diag. 68*)

        a. Jump from the board to the buck with the hips raised well above the shoulder level.

    b. Swing the legs to either side and extend the hip joint so that the body is fully extended well above a horizontal position. Forcefully push away from the buck, with the supporting arm, at the height of the ascent.

    c. Land in an even rear stand with the knees and hips slightly flexed and the arms extended sideward in a horizontal position.

Diag. 68

Diag. 69

SPOTTING SUGGESTIONS

    The buck should be at hip level or below for inexperienced vaulters. Spot the performer by standing to one side and by holding his supporting arm. Guide him through the stunt.

    2. *Front Vault* (2 points) (*Diag. 69*)

    a. Jump from the board to the buck with the fingers facing either left or right positions. The hips are raised to a position that causes the upper back to become parallel to the floor, as the upper body initiates a quarter turn to either side.

    b. After the hips have been raised and the quarter turn has been completed, the back is arched as one arm is extended sideward.

    c. The supporting arm remains on the horse to stabilize the landing. Finish in an even left side stand.

SPOTTING SUGGESTIONS

Same as the flank vault.

    3. *Squat Vault* (3 points) (*Diag. 70*)

    a. Jump from the board to the buck with the arms extended forward.

Diag. 70

Diag. 71

 b. Push off the buck vigorously when the hips rise above the shoulders and squat both legs between the arms.

 c. Continue holding the squat position until the body has passed over the horse. Straighten the body in a vertical position before landing.

Spotting Suggestions

Practice this movement on a mat by first assuming a front support position. During the vault, the spotter should assume a position at the side of the buck and grasp the student's arm as he is vaulting. This practice, plus adjusting the position of the student's upper back (to counteract under rotation) will insure a safe landing.

 4. *Straddle Vault* (2 points) (*Diag. 71*)

  a. Jump from the board to the buck with the arms extended in front of the body.

  b. Push off the buck vigorously and straddle the legs as wide as possible.

  c. Extend the body in a vertical position before landing.

Spotting Suggestions

Adjust the height of the buck according to the level of the performer's hips. Spot by standing directly in front of the buck and by grasping the student's upper arms as he pushes off the buck. Be alert for under-rotation and the student's catching his toe on the outer surfaces of the apparatus (especially true when the buck is in the even position).

 B. Buck in Cross Position

  1. *Squat Vault* (3 points) (*Diag. 72*)

      a. Refer to the squat vault with the buck in the even position.

  2. *Straddle Vault* (2 points) (*Diag. 73*)

      a. Refer to the straddle vault with the buck in the even position.

Side Horse (suggested value 6 points)

1.-2. *Front and Rear Support* (2 points) (*Diag. 74*)

      a. The arms should be straight with the hands on the forward portion of the pommels.

      b. The performer should keep the arms in full extension while bracing the shoulders; the pupil should focus his sight on the saddle while in the front support and on his hips in the rear support.

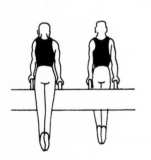

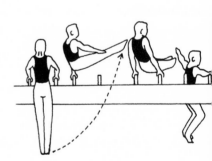

Diag. 74

Diag. 75

Diag. 76

SPOTTING SUGGESTIONS

Care should be exercised to have the performer's shoulders in a braced position. A "hunching" of the shoulders on the side horse could lead to postural defects.

3. *Flank Vault* (2 points) (*Diag. 75*)
   a. Stand facing the saddle with one hand on each pommel.
   b. Jump over the horse by shifting the weight of the body to either side. Raise the hips well above the horse and keep the supporting arm as straight as possible.
   c. Straighten the hips as the body passes over the horse and extend the free arm, as illustrated.
   d. Land in a semi-squat position with the arms extended horizontally to the side of the body (even rear stand).

SPOTTING SUGGESTIONS

Refer to the flank vault over the buck (Beginner Skills).

4. *Rear Vault* (2 points) (*Diag. 76*)
   a. Stand facing the saddle with one hand on each pommel.
   b. Jump over either pommel with the rear facing the saddle.
   c. Regrasp the pommel upon landing, as illustrated.

SPOTTING SUGGESTIONS

The spotter should stand facing the performer, in front of the left pommel. As the student vaults, support his left arm and upper back. Be sure to release his arm as he is shifting hands on the pommel.

Horizontal Bar (suggested value 12 points)

1. *Three Chins* (2 points) (*Diag. 77*)
   a. Hang on to the bar with both hands in a reverse grip position.
   b. Pull upward, with a straight body, so the chin is placed clearly above the bar.
   c. Return to the starting position with a smooth, even tempo and repeat three times.

SPOTTING SUGGESTIONS

The student may be assisted by stabilizing his hips.

2. *Three Toe Touches* (2 points) (*Diag. 78*)
   a. Hang on the bar with both hands in a regular grip position.

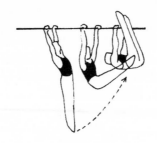
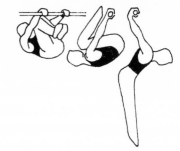

Diag. 77   **Diag. 78**   **Diag. 79**

   b. With a slight whip of the legs, bend at the hips and touch toes to the bar.

   c. Return to the starting position and repeat three times.

SPOTTING SUGGESTIONS

Spot by standing to the side of the student and controlling his body swing. The upper back should be given careful attention; in the event of a slip this portion of the body should be brought forward to prevent the pupil from landing on his back.

  3. *Skin the Cat* (3 points) (*Diag. 79*)

    a. Hang on the bar with a regular grip and raise the knees to the chest.

    b. Rotate the body backward as the feet pass between both arms and under the bar.

    c. Continue turning over backward until the body is fully stretched downward. Return to the starting position.

SPOTTING SUGGESTIONS

As the student rotates backward, place your right hand on his chest and your left hand on his back. On his return place your right hand behind his neck and your left hand on his chest. Stay with him until the circle is completed. This skill should first be practiced on a head-high bar.

  4. *Swing with Good Form* (3 points) (*Diag. 80*)

    a. From a hanging position with a regular grip, cast legs forward and upward. As the body reaches the front of the swing, stretch so a straight body position is assumed.

b. As the body is carried rearward, the hips are raised and the grip is shifted over the bar.

c. As the body swings forward, assume an arched position under the bar and pump forward and upward into a semi-piked position. Repeat this movement until a smooth, controlled swing results.

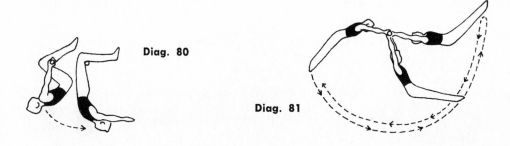

Diag. 80

Diag. 81

Spotting Suggestions

The instructor may aid the student by manually guiding him through the correct position. Spot by placing yourself beneath the bar and to one side. Watch the student and especially his grip, which would show the first sign of a slip. Have the pupil dismount at the end of his swing.

5. *Knee Hang* (2 points) (*Diag. 81*)

    a. Hang on the bar with a regular grip and raise the knees to the chest.

    b. Rotate the body backward as the feet pass between both arms and over the bar.

    c. Hook both legs over the bar, release hands from the bar and slowly extend the body backwards and downwards until a hanging position is assumed. Return to the starting position.

Spotting Suggestions

To insure a stronger knee grip have the student's feet in a dorsi-flexed position. When the pupil is ready to dismount, raise his chest, with constant support, and have him drop off the bar. This skill should first be practiced on a chest-high bar.

Parallel Bars (suggested value 15 points)

1. *Three Dips* (2 points) (*Diag. 82*)
   a. Support the body between the bars with straight arms.
   b. Lower the body between the bars so that the shoulders pass clearly below the elbows.
   c. Return to the starting position.

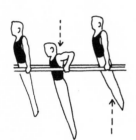

Diag. 82

Diag. 83

SPOTTING SUGGESTIONS

The performer's hips should be stabilized and care should be given to students whose arm strength is below par. These pupils are apt to fall forward and hyper-extend their shoulders. Overcome this situation by placing the bars to correspond with the shoulders or by supporting his chest with your hand. This skill should first be practiced on a chest-high bar.

2. *Walk the Length of the Bars* (3 points) (*Diag. 83*)
   a. Support the body between the bars with straight arms.
   b. Lean from left to right and walk the length of the bars.

SPOTTING SUGGESTIONS

Refer to No. 1, Three Dips.

3. *Cross Straddle Seats* (3 points) (*Diag. 84*)
   a. From a straight lower arm support, straddle both legs over both bars.

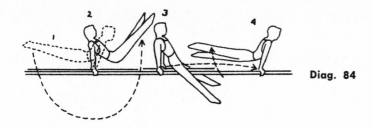

Diag. 84

b. Place the hands in front of the legs.

c. Swing both legs to the rear over both bars and replace them over both bars in front position.

SPOTTING SUGGESTIONS

Refer to No. 1, Three Dips.

4. *Swing in Lower Arm Support Position* (2 points) (*Diag. 85*)

   a. Swing legs forward so that the hips are clearly in front of the hands.

   b. Swing legs to the rear with emphasis on keeping the arms straight and maintaining the balance.

   c. Repeat this movement several times until a smooth, even swing results.

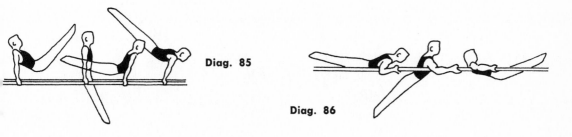

Diag. 85

Diag. 86

SPOTTING SUGGESTIONS

Progressively enlarge the scope of the swing on the low bars. Due to lack of arm and shoulder strength, the beginner will swing mainly from the hips with little or no rotary movement from the shoulders. As you start him on the correct procedure, careful observance should be given to a loss of control in both the forward and rear positions. Move and offer assistance if and when this occurs. This skill should first be practiced on waist-high bars.

5. *Swing in the Upper Arm Position* (2 points) (*Diag. 86*)

   a. Swing legs forward so that the hips are at bar level.

Diag. 87

b. Swing legs rearward so the hips are again at bar level.

c. Repeat this movement several times until a smooth, even swing results.

Tremendous friction is created by this move on the student's upper arms. A sweat shirt might be advisable in the early learning stages.

6. *Front Dismount* (3 points) (*Diag. 87*)

a. Swing forward so that the hips are clearly in front of the hands.

b. Swing rearward so that the feet clearly rise above the bars. As the body reaches the highest point of the swing the legs are placed over either bar.

c. At this point, both hands are placed upon one bar and the weight is transferred outward.

d. One hand remains holding the bar to stabilize the landing. Finish in an even right side stand.

You may spot the student by standing in an even left side stand and supporting the pupil's right arm as he passes over the bar; follow through until he is standing. This skill should first be practiced on waist-high bars.

Still Rings (suggested value 13 points)

1. *Swing with Good Form* (3 points) (*Diag. 88*)

a. From a hanging position, swing backward and forward with straight arms. The point of rotation should be the shoulders.

SPOTTING SUGGESTIONS

Stand to the side of the pupil and assist him by applying pressure to his back while he is in the forward position and on his chest while he is in the backward position. Be prepared to control the student's momentum if the rings' angle goes too far beyond the perpendicular.

2. *Bird's Nest Hang* (3 points) (*Diag. 89*)
   a. From a hanging position, swing the legs between both arms. Hook both feet, one in each ring, and arch the body backward, as illustrated. Hold this position for three seconds and return to the starting position.

SPOTTING SUGGESTIONS

As illustrated.

3. *Inverted Hang in Piked Position* (4 points) (*Diag. 90*)
   a. From a hanging position, swing both legs between the rings and hold for three seconds, as illustrated. The student's eyes should be focused on his legs which are parallel to the floor.

SPOTTING SUGGESTIONS

As illustrated.

4. *Bent Arm Hang in Piked Position* (3 points) (Diag. 91)
   a. From a hanging position, pull the body upwards so the bases of the rings are close to the shoulders.
   b. Raise the legs, and maintain the right angle position for three seconds.

Diag. 88   **Diag. 89**   **Diag. 90**   **Diag. 91**

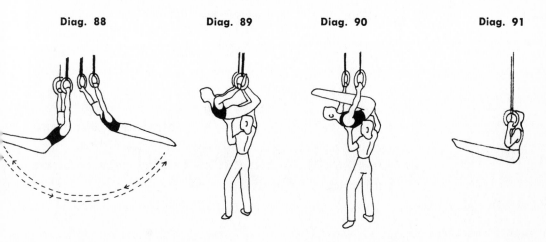

Most students will find this position very difficult in their early stages of skill development Therefore, it would be advisable to assist the pupil by supporting his legs while controlling his upper back until he gets the feel of the final position.

Tumbling (suggested value 9 points)

1. *Shoulder Roll* (2 points) (*Diag. 92*)
   a. Step forward with either leg and extend the corresponding arm downward with the fingers extended toward the body.
   b. Lean forward into the roll and absorb the shock of the fall by slapping the mat with the extended hand.
   c. Only the extended arm, the upper back, the opposing hip and knee will make contact with the mat as the performer rolls over.

Diag. 92

   d. This roll is performed diagonally across the back from either shoulder to the opposing hip and knee.

This skill may be practiced from a kneeling position in those cases where students are having a difficult time adjusting to its execution.

2. *Forward Roll* (2 points) (*Diag. 93*)
   a. Assume a semi-squat position with both arms extended forward. Push off the mat with both feet and lean forward with both arms reaching downward toward the mat.
   b. Absorb the shock of the fall by bending the arms as the body weight is placed upon them.

Diag. 93

c. Duck the head just before it contacts the floor.

d. Roll forward with a rounded back, by placing the neck, upper back, lower back and seat on the mat. Once the neck is flexed, the knees are brought into the chest which promotes the rounded back position.

e. As the weight of the body is relieved from the hands, they are removed from the mat and placed on the knees to insure a tight tuck position. The roll is completed when the performer is standing erect.

SPOTTING SUGGESTIONS

This movement may be practiced from a deep squat position which will put the performer closer to the mat. As the student starts the roll you can assist by placing your hand behind his neck and guiding him through the maneuver. If he is having trouble rolling, have him place his hands rather close to his body and have him stay high on his toes; this position will alleviate some of the trouble. Furthermore you can have the student lie on his back, in a tuck position, knees drawn tightly to the chest, and practice rocking back and forth.

3. *Backward Roll* (2 points) (*Diag. 94*)

a. From a standing position, with the wrists extended and placed just over the ears, squat to a sitting position and roll backward. The knees remain flexed throughout the roll.

b. The neck is flexed and the arms are extended as the body weight passes over the head and on to the hands.

c. The arms continue their action (extension) as the weight passes on to the feet.

Diag. 94

Spotting Suggestions

As the student rolls back, place your hand behind his neck to help lessen pressure on the neck. If he is having trouble with the move have him start in a squat position with his neck fully flexed; then have him sit back and push vigorously, being sure to maintain the tuck position.

4. *Cartwheel* (3 points) (*Diag. 95*)

   a. Stand erect with legs about shoulder-width apart and the arms extended horizontally. Raise the leg that corresponds to the direction of the cartwheel.

   b. Step and lean in the direction of the move. Push with the leading foot and kick the rear leg over the head as the hands make contact with the mat.

   c. The body should pass through a handstand position with the legs straddled as wide as possible.

   d. Place the first foot that makes contact with the mat as close as possible. The legs and arms remain straight throughout the skill.

   e. Return to the starting position.

Diag. 95

Spotting Suggestions

You may assist the student by standing to his rear; when he is about to place his left hand on the floor, support his left side with

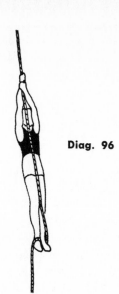

Diag. 96

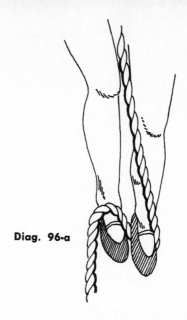

Diag. 96-a

your right hand (in supine position). As he kicks up to the handstand, place your left hand on his right side and guide him through the remainder of the skill. The beginning gymnast, due to lack of arm and shoulder strength, will most likely have some trouble in performing this skill; however, with constant practice, a fair degree of execution may be obtained.

Rope Climb (suggested value 8 points)

1. *Climb 10 Feet with Clinch* (8 points) (*Diag. 96*)
   a. From a hanging position at the base of the rope, raise the knees and place the rope on the outer edge of one foot and across the instep of the other as illustrated.
   b. Climb upward hand over hand as far as the clinch will allow. Release the clinch, raise the knees to the chest and reclinch. Continue climbing in this manner until the ten-foot mark is reached with the hands.

SPOTTING SUGGESTIONS

The student should be made to demonstrate his clinching ability before starting his ascent. If he can support himself on the rope without using his hands for support, he can safely climb to the prescribed height. During the descent have the student maintain the clinch (knees extended) and apply a hand-under-hand arm action. A mat should always be used under the rope.

Stunts (suggested value 9 points)

1. *Wheel Barrow* (2 points) (*Diag. 97*)
    a. Assume the position as illustrated. This exercise may be employed as a racing game utilizing two or more teams.
2. *Monkey Walks* (2 points) (*Diag. 98*)
    a. Assume the position, as illustrated, making sure that the legs and arms are held straight. This exercise may also be used in the form of a racing game.

Diag. 97

Diag. 99

Diag. 98

3. *Three-Man Pyramids* (2 points) (*Diag. 99*)
    a. The bottom men always assume their positions first.
    b. The top man secures his balance with the aid of his arms until his feet are in place. These movements are very effective with large groups.
4. *Log Rolls* (3 points) (*Diag. 100*)
    a. Three men assume a hand and knee position about 18 inches apart. By pushing with the toes and arms, No. 2 jumps over No. 1 while No. 1 rolls under No. 2. As No. 2 lands and rolls under No. 3, No. 3 jumps over No. 2, etc. The rolling action should be combined with the leap to insure fast and continuous movement.

Diag. 100

Spotting Suggestions

Have the pupils walk through the maneuver before they attempt the stunt. Be sure that each student can demonstrate an individual log roll with the body in a fully extended position.

Novice

Skills

VI

Floor Exercise (suggested value 12 points)

    1. *Three Point Balance* (1 point)
      (*Diag. 101*)
       a. Assume the "tip-up" position (re-
          fer to Beginner Skills, Free Calis-
          thenics No. 2).
       b. Slowly lean forward, while main-
          taining a balanced position, and
          place the uppermost portion of

Diag. 101

Diag. 102

Diag. 103

the forehead on the mat. The head is placed about 12 inches in front of the hands.

SPOTTING SUGGESTIONS

Refer to Beginner Skills, Floor Exercise No. 2.

2. *Single Leg Circles* (3) (2 points) (*Diag. 102*)
   a. Assume the starting position, as illustrated.
   b. Swing the left leg (circular path) under the left hand and right hand. Maintain pivot foot under buttocks.
   c. Replace the hands, kick off the right foot and swing the left leg under the right foot back to starting position.
3. *Jump to High Straddle* (2 points) (*Diag. 103*)
   a. Jump upward, as high as possible, using a full arm elevation for lift.
   b. Raise both legs as high as possible in front of the body in a wide straddle position and touch both toes at the same time.
   c. Return to standing position.

SPOTTING SUGGESTIONS

Have the student execute this move in a slight pike. This will prevent his falling backward from lack of body control.

4. *Lunge Position* (1 point) (*Diag. 104*)
   a. Assume the position illustrated, emphasizing elevated arm position.
5. *From a Front Support, Squat Through to Back Support* (2 points) (*Diag. 105*)
   a. From a front support position, push off with both feet, raise hips and bring the knees into the chest.
   b. Squat both legs between arms without touching the matted area between the hands.
   c. Slide legs forward on the mat and assume a rear support.

Diag. 104

Diag. 105

Spotting Suggestions

Have the pupil practice this skill by first jumping to a full squat position. This type of training will prevent "forearm splints" which are brought about by constantly hitting the floor with the palms of the hands (as seen in position No. 3).

6. *Scale on Either Leg* (2 points) (*Diag. 106*)
    a. From a standing position, extend both arms over head and raise either leg to the rear as high as it will go.
    b. Maintain a locked position in the hip as the upper body is lowered into position.
    c. The student should lower his upper body only as low as arched back position will allow. At no time should the hips be higher than the head or the foot.

Spotting Suggestions

The instructor may place the student in the correct position by holding his chest and leg.

Diag. 106

Diag. 107

7. *Forward Roll* (1) (1 point) (*Diag. 107*)
    a. Step and kick into forward roll. Refer to Beginner Skills, Tumbling No. 2.
8. *Supported Handstand* (*and Headstand*) (1 point) (*Diags. 108-109*)

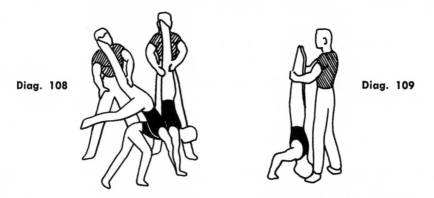

Diag. 108   **Diag. 109**

Handstand with Spotter
a. Bend forward and place hands on the floor about shoulder-width apart. The hands should be flat on the floor, fingers forward and spread apart.
b. One leg should be bent (close to chest) and the other leg should be straight and extended to the rear.
c. Push with the bent leg and swing the straight leg over head. The legs are brought together in the handstand position and the eyes are focused between the hands. Try to maintain a balanced position by manipulating the fingers and shoulders in accordance with the shifting body weight.

Aside from spotting from a lateral plane, you can also assist by standing directly in front of the student. Place one of your legs in front of either shoulder (make contact), then have the pupil kick up. While supporting him in the balance, slowly move the leg that is supporting the student forward until the shoulders are in a fully extended position. This position is totally unfamiliar to the youth and one that he should practice constantly for successful execution of the hand balance.

Headstand with Spotter

  a. Assume three-point balance position (*see* Novice Skills, Floor Exercise No. 1)
  b. Slowly raise hips and legs overhead while maintaining a balanced position.

The instructor may catch the student's legs and guide him into the correct position. The student may also use a padded wall to keep him from over-balancing if an instructor is not available.

Vaulting Box (with beat board; suggested value 12 points)

A. Box in Even Position (medium height)

  1. *Flank Vault* (1 point) (*Diag. 110*)
     a. Refer to Beginner Skills, Buck in Even Position No. 1.
  2. *Front Vault* (1 point) (*Diag. 111*)
     a. Refer to Beginner Skills, Buck in Even Position No. 2.

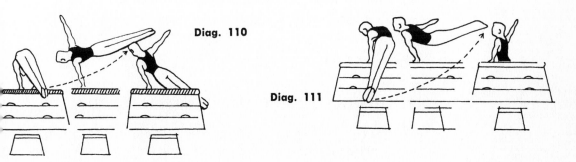

Diag. 110

Diag. 111

3. *Squat Vault* (1 point) (*Diag. 112*)
    a. Refer to Beginner Skills, Buck in Even Position No. 3.
4. *Straddle Vault* (1 point) (*Diag. 113*)
    a. Refer to Beginner Skills, Buck in Even Position No. 4.

B. Box in Cross Position (medium height)

1. *Front Vault from Saddle* (2 points) (*Diag. 114*)
    a. Refer to Beginner Skills, Buck No. 2.
2. *Straddle Vault from Neck* (2 points) (*Diag. 115*)
    a. Refer to Beginner Skills, Buck No. 4.
3. *Squad Vault from the Neck* (2 points) (*Diag. 116*)
    a. Refer to Beginner Skills, Buck No. 3.
4. *Forward Roll* (2 points) (*Diag. 117*)
    a. From a controlled run, dive off the board with the head up and the arms leading.
    b. Absorb the shock of the leap, with the arms, by bending them at the moment of contact with the box. The chin is tucked into the chest, at this point, to avoid hitting the head.
    c. The knees are brought into the chest and the hands clasp the lower legs just below the knee.
    d. The performer dismounts by rolling to his feet and jumping off the horse to an erect standing position.

SPOTTING SUGGESTIONS

The instructor may manually assist the performer by grasping his upper arm, during the leap, with one hand and supporting his neck with the other hand. This technique of spotting should keep the student over the box and help him to roll. The vaulting box should only be slightly above hip level. In the early stages of learning this skill, guide the student through the maneuver because the pupil has a tendency to roll to one side. In doing so he might possibly fall off the apparatus. It is advisable to have a spotter on both sides of the box.

NOTE: The long horse may be substituted for the vaulting box.

Side Horse (suggested value 10 points) (*Diag. 118*)

1. *From a Front Support Over Saddle: cut right leg over right pommel and under right hand; repeat with left leg to the*

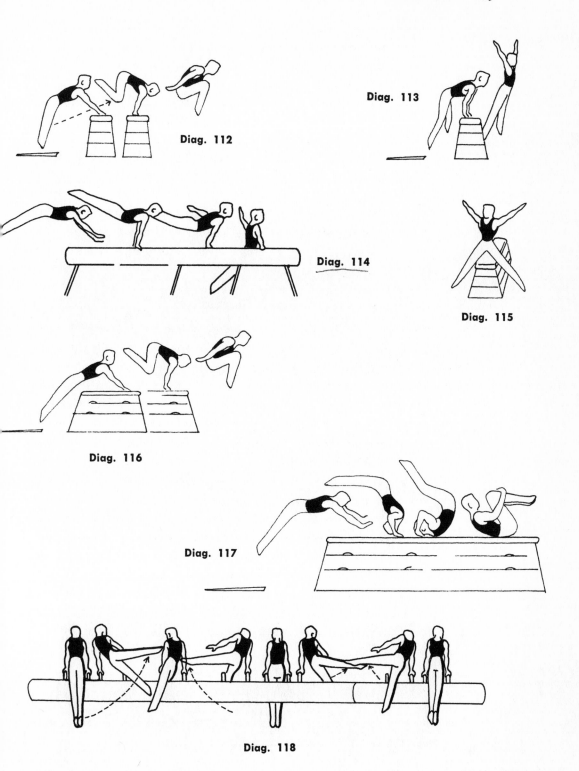

Diag. 112

Diag. 113

Diag. 114

Diag. 115

Diag. 116

Diag. 117

Diag. 118

left side to a rear support. Cut right leg back over the right pommel and under the right hand and repeat with the left leg on left side to a front support. (3 points)

a. Assume a front support position.
b. Swing the right leg laterally under right hand and over right pommel and regrasp the right pommel with the right hand.
c. Continue the swing and raise the left leg laterally under the left hand and over the left pommel and regrasp the left pommel.
d. Without stopping, swing the right leg back over the right pommel and the left leg back over the left pommel.
e. This is a lateral movement that starts in a front support and ends in a front support.

SPOTTING SUGGESTIONS

The wearing of gymnastic trousers will prevent knee abrasions that are caused by the constant sliding of the legs on the side horse (especially in the early stages of learning).

2. *Travel from the Croup to the Saddle or Reverse* (3 points) (*Diag. 119*)

a. Jump to a front support position over the neck.
b. Swing the left leg under the left hand. Replace the left hand on the neck.
c. Swing the right leg over the saddle and transfer the body weight from the neck to the left pommel.
d. Swing the left leg to the rear and place the left hand, behind the right hand, on the left pommel.
e. Lean to left, with both hands on the left pommel, and swing the right leg laterally over the right pommel.
f. Place the right hand on the right pommel and finish in a front support position over the saddle. The performer may also travel, in the same manner from the saddle to the neck.

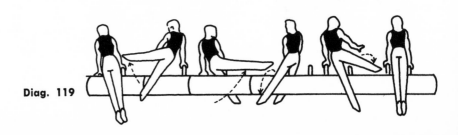

Diag. 119

Due to the nature of this apparatus, students have a tendency to over-practice a skill. Often this can lead to forearm "splints," caused by the constant handling of the pommels. This can be avoided by reducing the repetitions.

3. *From an Even Front Stand with Right Hand on Left Pommel, Under Outer Grip, and the Left Hand on the Neck: jump to a front support position and immediate half turn to the left and pass left leg over right pommel to straddle support (back stecklie action). (2 points) (Diag. 120)*
   a. Stand facing the neck with the right hand on the left pommel in an outer grip.
   b. Jump to an immediate half turn to the left.
   c. Finish in a rear support, as illustrated, on the saddle.

Diag. 120

Diag. 121

4. *Feint with Either Leg and Execute a Single Rear Dismount to an Even Right Side Stand. (2 points) (Diag. 121)*
   a. Jump to front support over the saddle with regular grip.
   b. Feint the right leg over the wrist of the right hand, as illustrated.
   c. Swing the right leg rearward, in a circular path, both legs joining in the rear and continuing to swing.
   d. Both legs swing under the left hand while the seat passes over the horse. The right hand remains as the pivot point until the cross side stand is maintained.

After feinting with the right leg, move in and grasp the student's right wrist and forearm and guide him through the rear vault.

Horizontal Bar (suggested value 13 points)

1. *Five Chins with Reverse Grip* (2 points) (*Diag. 122*)
   a. Refer to Beginner Skills, Horizontal Bar No. 1.
2. *Five Toe Touches with Regular Grip* (3 points) (*Diag. 123*)
   a. Refer to Beginner Skills, Horizontal Bar No. 2.
3. *Cast with Good Form* (3 points) (*Diag. 124*)
   a. Jump to a hanging position on the bar with a slight swing.
   b. Arch the back at the rear of the swing and snap the ankles to the bar as the body swings forward.
   c. Shoot the feet away from the bar (upward and outward) by extending at the hip joint.
   d. Swing to the rear and dismount at the bottom of the swing.

SPOTTING SUGGESTIONS

The instructor may aid the student by manipulating his shoulders and legs to insure the correct body positions.

Careful consideration should always be given to the manner in which the student releases the bar for the dismount. The dismount should always be performed at the "stopping point" of the rearward swing.

4. *Back Hip Circle Mount* (3 points) (*Diag. 125*)
   a. Grasp the bar *at chest level* with bent arms.
   b. Raise the legs off the mat and pull the bar into the abdomen as the body turns over backward, head extended.
   c. Continue pulling with the arms until a balanced position, over the bar, is assumed.
   d. Straighten the body and assume a front support position.

SPOTTING SUGGESTIONS

The instructor may aid the student by guiding his shoulders and hips into position, as illustrated.

5. *From a Support, Forward Hip Circle to a Hang* (2 points) (*Diag. 126*)
   a. Assume a front support position on a medium high bar.
   b. Bend forward, from the hip, and roll over the bar to a hanging position.
   c. The rolling action should be smooth and continuous.

Diag. 122

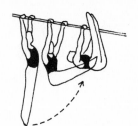

Diag. 123

Diag. 124

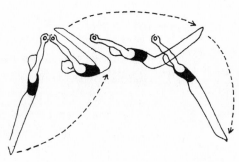

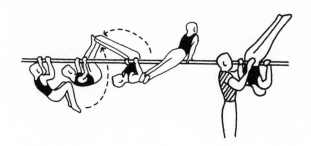

Diag. 125

Diag. 126

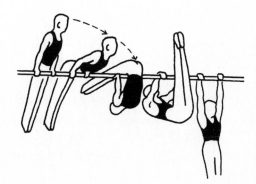

You may grasp the student's right wrist with your right hand and place your left hand on the pupil's neck as he is halfway through the circle (No. 3).

Parallel Bars (suggested value 16 points)

1. *From an Even Front Stand, Scissor Mount to a Straddle Seat* (2 points) *(Diag. 127)*
   a. From an even front stand with a mixed grip, jump and put both legs over the far bar and scissor the leg that corresponds to the under-grip.
   b. Cross the over-grip hand over the under-grip hand and re-grasp the bar as the body turns below the bars.
   c. The shoulder of the under-grip hand should be forced above the bar as the legs straddle both bars. The completed movement represents a quarter turn between the bars, from a hanging position to a straddle lower arm support position.

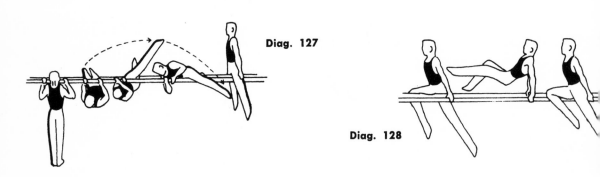

Diag. 127

Diag. 128

The instructor may manually guide the student through the correct body positions.

This is especially true in position No. 3. At this point the student, in most cases, will appreciate your direct assistance which can be administered by giving support to the chest and thus helping him through the "crisis" of the move.

2. *Arch Seat on One Bar* (1 point) (*Diag. 128*)
   a. From a lower arm support, swing both legs over either bar and assume the position illustrated.
3. *Two Swinging Dips* (2 points) (*Diag. 129*)
   a. Obtain a slight swing in a lower arm support position.
   b. Bend the arms at the rear of the swing so the shoulders are clearly below the level of the elbows.
   c. Swing forward in the dip position and straighten the arms.

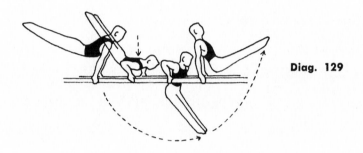

Diag. 129

SPOTTING SUGGESTIONS

Students lacking in upper body strength are usually prone to loosing their support in position No. 4. You can assist by placing your hand on the pupil's upper back as he starts to ascend above the bars.

4. *Swing from a Lower Arm Support* (2 points) (*Diag. 130*)
   a. Refer to Beginner Skills, Parallel Bars No. 4.
5. *From Cross Front Stand at Near End, Jump to a Glide Pike (with a tap).* (2 points) (*Diag. 131*)
   a. From a cross front stand, grasp the bars and jump backward with hips raised.
   b. Swing forward in a semi-piked position.
   c. Tap the toes on the mat at the peak of the forward swing.
   d. Swing backward, after tapping, in a deep piked position, as illustrated.

Diag. 130

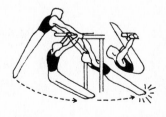

Diag. 131

Guide the student through the maneuver from the first few times. If the novice has a tendency to go into a skin-the-cat motion on his return from the tap, you can directly assist him to a safe landing.

6. *From an Upper Arm Support, Swing to Piked Inverted Hang and Kip to a Straddle Seat* (3 points) (*Diag. 132*)

   a. From an upper arm support, swing the body to a deep piked position above the bars.

   b. "Snap" the legs upward and forward, away from the face. The hips are held well above the bars and the arms should be straight.

   c. As the shoulders rise off the bars, the legs are straddled as wide as possible.

   d. Assume a straddle seat position.

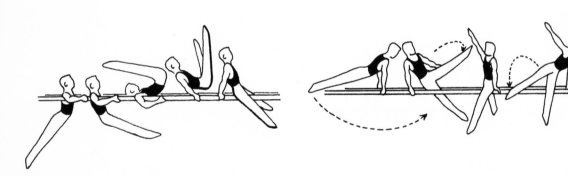

Diag. 132   **Diag. 133**

SPOTTING SUGGESTIONS

The instructor may aid the student by reaching below the bars and placing one hand on his hips and one hand on his upper back at the moment of "snap."

7. *Walk Off Dismount to an Even Left Side Stand* (2 points) (*Diag. 133*)

   a. From a lower arm support position, obtain a slight swing.

   b. On the forward swing, place the left leg over the right bar.

   c. Remove the right hand from the right bar and swing the right leg rearward over the right bar. Push the body away from both bars with the left hand.

S<small>POTTING</small> S<small>UGGESTIONS</small>

Stand to the side of the student and be prepared to stabilize him from the front if he should catch his right foot on the bar (No. 4) or from the rear, should he over-rotate (No. 5).

8. *Rear Dismount to an Even Left Side Stand* (2 points) *(Diag. 134)*

   a. Swing forward until the hips are clearly above the bars.

Diag. 134

   b. Place the hips and legs over either bar while the body still has forward motion. Remove the hand from the bar that is in opposition to the direction of the dismount and grasp the bar with the same hand that the body is passing over. The change of grip is made behind the back and for a moment both hands are on the same bar.

   c. As the body descends, the outside hand is removed from the bar and extended, as illustrated.

S<small>POTTING</small> S<small>UGGESTIONS</small>

The instructor may hold the wrist of the hand that corresponds to the direction of the dismount. This method of spotting will assure the student's flight over the bar and aid in his stability upon landing. Have the student first practice the skill on chest-high bars.

Still Rings (suggested value 11 points)

1. *Swing to Piked Inverted Hang* (2 points) *(Diag. 135)*

   a. From a hanging position on *medium high* rings, obtain a swing by pumping the legs forward and backward.

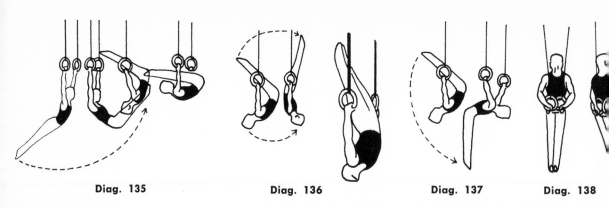

Diag. 135   **Diag. 136**   **Diag. 137**   **Diag. 138**

    b. On the forward swing, increase the piked position and assume the inverted piked hang. Hold this position for three seconds—*see* Beginner Skills, Still Rings No. 3.

2. *From a Piked Inverted Hang, Open to a Vertical or Inverted Hang* (3 points) (*Diag. 136*)

    a. Swing to piked inverted hang.

    b. Slowly raise legs and lower back until a straight body position is assumed, as illustrated. The body should be straightened slowly for maximum control.

SPOTTING SUGGESTIONS

You should assist the student by controlling his chest and upper legs. Often this position will upset a student's equilibrium, requiring that he be manually held in position.

3. *Skin the Cat* (2 points) (*Diag. 137*)

    a. Swing through piked inverted hang position on the *medium high* rings.

    b. Continue turning over backwards until the body is completely extended. Hold this position for three seconds and return to hang.

SPOTTING SUGGESTIONS

Assist the student by supporting his back at the start and his chest at the completion of the half turn. On his return, while supporting his chest, place your other hand behind his neck (causing the neck to assume a flexed position) and guide him through the maneuver.

4. *Support with the Rings Behind the Back* (2 points) (*Diag. 138*)

    a. Assist the student in pulling to a lower arm support.

    b. Place the rings behind the back with the palms of the hands facing rearward as illustrated. Hold this support position for three seconds and return to hang.

Control the student's legs and in the event the support gives way, slowly lower him to the floor.

5. *Forward Single Leg Cut Dismount* (2 points) (*Diag. 139*)
    a. Swing to piked inverted hang position on *the medium high rings*.
    b. Rock backward and forward. On forward rock, cut one leg over corresponding wrist and grip.
    c. Continue holding on with the supporting arm until the body is in position for the landing as illustrated.

Diag. 139

Support the student by controlling the back of his neck. If he should under-rotate, push him in a forward direction.

Tumbling (suggested value 14 points)

1. *Forward Roll with Slight Dive* (2 points) (*Diag. 140*)
    a. Refer to Beginner Skills, Tumbling No. 2.
2. *Back Roll in Piked Position* (2 points) (*Diag. 141*)
    a. Refer to Beginner Skills, Tumbling No. 3.

Diag. 140

Diag. 141

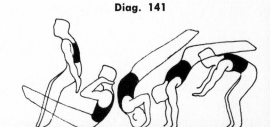

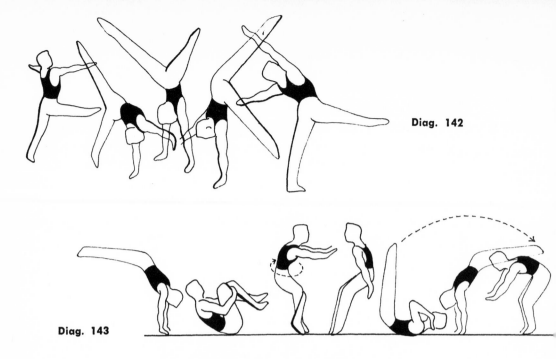

Diag. 142

Diag. 143

3. *Two Cartwheels* (3 points) (*Diag. 142*)
   a. Refer to Beginner Skills, Tumbling No. 4.
4. *Forward Roll and Cross Over to Backward Roll* (2 points) (*Diag. 143*)
   a. Refer to Beginner Skills, Tumbling Nos. 2 and 3.
   b. Cross the legs, as illustrated, in either direction, and perform a half turn in the direction that corresponds to the crossed legs. This will allow the performer to combine both tricks in a smooth pattern.
5. *Round-Off* (3 points) (*Diag. 144*)
   a. From a stand or a short run, step and hop on either leg while lifting the opposite leg toward the chest. The hands during this hurdle are raised directly over the head.
   b. Place both hands on the mat, one in front of the other, and kick both feet overhead one at a time.
   c. As the performer passes through a handstand position, his legs are joined.

Diag. 144

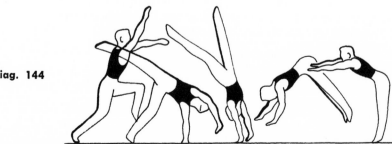

The first quarter of the turn is completed when the hands are placed on the mat. The second quarter of the turn is completed as the performer passes through the handstand position. Thus, a half turn is performed by means of a round-off.

d. The joined legs are whipped down, close to the hands, as a result of the power from the initial kick.

e. The performer lands in a standing position with a slight bend in the hips.

Spotting Suggestions

This trick may be taught by teaching the performer to finish a "cartwheel" on both feet at the same time. The instructor may hold the student's waist with both hands for spotting. Also, to insure the execution as a complete half turn, which often is over- as well as under-turned, have the student during position No. 2, place both hands on the mat in a position parallel to his shoulder. To perform this maneuver, the student must avoid rotating his upper body, until his hands are secured in position.

6. *Round-Off and Back Roll* (2 points) (*Diag. 145*)
    a. This is a combination of Diag. 144 and Diag. 94.
    b. There shouldn't be any stopping between parts.

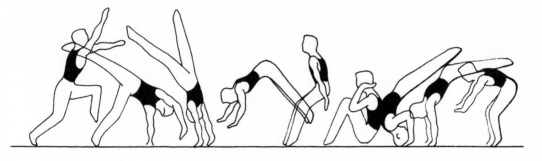

Diag. 145

Rope Climbing (suggested value 4 points)

1. *Climb 15 Feet with Hands and Feet* (4 points)
    a. Refer to Beginner Skills, Rope Climb No. 1.

Stunts (suggested value 8 points)

1. *Log Rolls* (1 point)
   a. Refer to Beginner Skills, Stunts No. 4.
2. *Monkey Shines* (2 points) (*Diag. 146*)
   a. Nos. 2 and 3 stand facing each other with No. 3 standing behind 1. No. 1 rolls under 2 and No. 2 straddle jumps over 1. Upon landing, No. 2 rolls under 3 and No. 3 straddle jumps over 2. After each performer rolls he must stand and turn around as quickly as possible in preparation for a straddle jump.
   b. Repeat this combination seven or eight times.

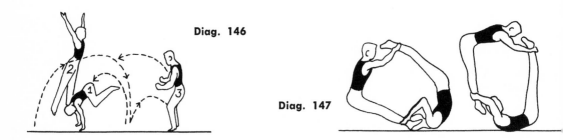

Diag. 146

Diag. 147

SPOTTING SUGGESTIONS

Have the students practice a forward roll in an extremely tucked position.

3. *Two-Man Forward Rolls* (3 points) (*Diag. 147*)
   a. Assume the position illustrated with one man on his back and the other on his feet.
   b. Roll forward with control using each other's feet to absorb the shock of the fall.

SPOTTING SUGGESTIONS

As the top man makes his descent from the roll, follow him through the turn by supporting the back of his neck and controlling the wrist. This will insure his completing the turn safely.

4. *Four-Man Pyramids* (2 points) (*Diags. 148, 149, 150*)

Diag. 148

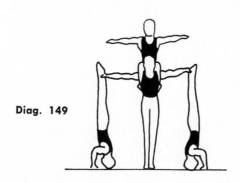

Diag. 149

Diag. 150

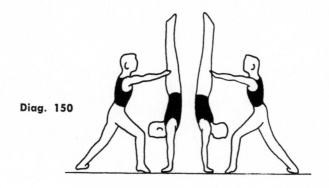

a. In each case both men in the middle assume their positions first. The outside men assist the inside men and later assume their positions.

Intermediate

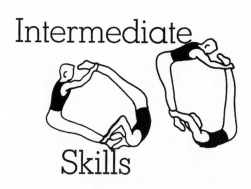

Skills

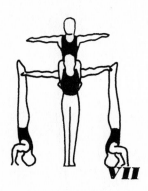

F**loor Exercise** (suggested value 18 points)

1. *Head Balance* (3 points) (*Diag. 151*)
   a. Refer to Novice Skills, Free Calisthenics No. 8.
2. *Snap-Down* (2 points) (*Diag. 152*)
   a. Kick to three-quarter handstand or handstand position.
   b. Hyper-extend the hips and go

Diag. 151

Diag. 152

Diag. 153

into an immediate action-reaction movement by flexing the hips (snapping type motion of the legs) while pushing off from the floor with the hands.

   c.   The feet make contact with the floor about six inches from the area where the hands were during the handstand. This is a lead-up trick for a back handspring.

SPOTTING SUGGESTIONS

You can help the performer by holding his legs in a handstand and casting them in the correct position for the snap-down. Your command to the student should be: "arch, pike and push."

   3. *Back Roll to Straddle Stand, Hands in Horizontal Position* (2 points) (*Diag. 153*)

     a. Refer to Novice Skills, Tumbling No. 2. This movement is completed in a wide straddle stand position, as illustrated.

   4. *High "V" with Straight Arm Support* (1 point)

     a. Refer to Beginner Skills, Floor Exercise No. 7b.

   5a. *Cartwheel, Quarter Turn and Forward Roll* (3 points) (*Diag. 154: a-e-; i and j*)

   5b. *Scale, Kick to Handstand and Forward Roll* (*no hold*) (3 points) (*Diag. 154 f-j*)

(left to right)

Diag. 154

a. This exercise is a combination of exercises that have been illustrated and described in the Beginner and Novice Skills. However, it should be mentioned that each part or trick must be combined with the next trick smoothly and that the "scale" is held for three seconds (*see* Diags. e-j).

6. *Neck Kip* (4 points) (*Diag. 155*)
   a. Roll backward on shoulders with the hips in a hyper-piked position. The elbows should be held high with the fingers facing inward toward the shoulders.
   b. Snap upward, by extending at the hips, and pushing with the hands against the floor (50° leg thrust, approximately).
   c. Continue pushing with the hands until both legs have landed on the floor. The back should be arched so the feet land, as closely as possible, to the area where the hands were placed.

Diag. 155

d. Upon landing, the hips are forced forward, the head is held back and the arms remain raised above the head.

SPOTTING SUGGESTIONS

The performer may be aided by supporting his lower back as he snaps into the arched position.

Long Horse (suggested value 8 points)

Horse in Cross Position at Standard Height

1. *Straddle Vault from the Neck* (3.5 points)
   a. Refer to Novice Skills, Vaulting Box (B) No. 2.

2. *Squat Vault from the Neck* (4.5 points)
   a. Refer to Novice Skills, Vaulting Box (B) No. 3.

Side Horse (suggested value 16 points)

1. *From an Even Front Stand Facing the Saddle, Hold Pommels
   with Over-grip and Flank Mount to Rear Support* (2 points)
   (*Diag. 156*)
   a. Stand facing the saddle with both hands on the pommels.
   b. Jump over either side of the horse with hips extended side-
      ward and supporting arm close to the ribs.
   c. Finish in even rear support position.

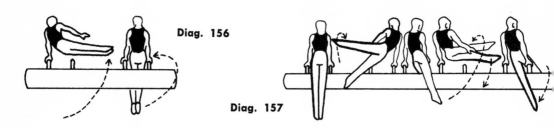

Diag. 156

Diag. 157

SPOTTING SUGGESTIONS

If the student has trouble initiating the mount you can either
lower the horse or provide him with an inclined board to start on.
Raising the performer's position often will enhance the learning
situation.

2. *From Front Support Over Saddle, Execute One Regular
   Scissor on Either Side* (2 points) (*Diag. 157*)
   a. From a front support, swing the left leg under the left hand
      and over left pommel. Replace the left hand on the left
      pommel.
   b. Swing both legs well above the horse on the right side.
      Push off the right pommel with the right hand, lean to the
      left and cross both legs to opposite sides of the horse. The
      rear leg swings over the front leg as the cross is made.
      Finish in a straddle support.

SPOTTING SUGGESTIONS

The wearing of gymnastics pants will prevent leg and knee abrasions.

3. *Travel from Croup to Neck or Reverse* (3 points)
    a. Refer to Novice Skills, Side Horse No. 2.
4. *From a Front Support Over Saddle: swing right leg over right pommel and under right hand to straddle support; repeat with the left leg to the left side to a rear support. Swing right leg back over right pommel and under right hand to straddle support and repeat with the left leg to the left side to a front support.* (2 points)
    a. Refer to Novice Skills, Side Horse No. 1.
5. *From a Front Support Over Saddle: swing the left leg over the left pommel and under the left hand and continue swinging the left leg over the right pommel and under the right hand to a front support (single leg full circle).* (3 points) (Diag. 158)
    a. As the left leg passes over the left pommel, the body weight must immediately be transferred to the right hand; the weight then must be transferred back to the left hand when the leg passes over the right pommel.
    b. Keep the center of gravity over the center of the horse and push vigorously with the left hand when the left leg completes the last cut.
    c. End in the even front support position.

Diag. 158

SPOTTING SUGGESTIONS

If the student pumps or extends the left leg while in the straddle support position (figures 2 and 3), he will find it very easy to arrive at the final front support position. It would be advisable to have the boy wear pants while performing this skill to avoid knee and leg abrasions.

6. *From a Front Support Over Croup: swing the left leg over the right pommel and under the left hand and immediately swing the right leg over croup and under right hand to rear support to immediate rear vault dismount with a quarter turn to even right side stand.* (4 points) *(Diag. 159)*

Diag. 159
(left to right)

    a. As the left leg passes over the right pommel, shift the body weight completely over the right hand. Regrab the right pommel as soon as the leg cuts over and reshift the weight back to the left hand.

    b. While supporting the body weight with the left hand, pass the right leg over the croup to the rear support, push with the right hand, pike at the hips, look over your left shoulder and execute a rear vault with a quarter turn to a cross right side stand.

SPOTTING SUGGESTIONS

The pumping or extending of both legs in the rear support position (figure 3) will enhance the student's execution of the move. In spotting this move, stand in a cross front stand (croup end) and as the performer swings the right leg over the croup, move in and support him around the waist while he concludes the quarter turn.

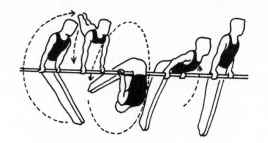

Diag. 160

Horizontal Bar (suggested value 13 points)

1. *Cast and Continue to Swing* (1 point)
   a. Refer to Novice Skills, Horizontal Bar No. 3.
2. *From a Front Support, Swing to Back Hip Circle to a Front Support* (3 points) (*Diag. 160*)
   a. Assume a front support position.
   b. Cast backward and swing the legs downward and bring the abdomen into the bar.
   c. Flex the hips, lean backward and circle the bar, as illustrated.
   d. Raise the chest and assume a front support position.

SPOTTING SUGGESTIONS

Have the student practice the skill on the low bar. Hold his right wrist while standing in front of him and reaching under the bar, and maintain his rotary movement with the other hand by supporting the "hamstring" area of his legs.

3. *From a Hang, Cast and Forward Single Leg Circle Mount* (3 points) (*Diag. 161*)
   a. From a hanging position, cast and obtain a swing.
   b. On the forward swing, bring the right leg between the hands and over the bar and pull with the arms.
   c. Swing the left leg downward and pull the shoulders over the bar.

Diag. 161

SPOTTING SUGGESTIONS

Guide the pupil by controlling his lower leg and giving him support on the upper back. On the forward swing the leg may be brought to the outside of the hand as well as between the hands.

4. *Single Leg Circle, Forward, Backward* (4 points) (*Diags. 162, 163*)

Forward

    a. Perform a single leg circle mount to support on the bar.

    b. With a reverse grip, place the bar behind the knee and roll forward. The thigh of the back leg is held against the bar and the upper body is stretched upward as the body falls forward.

    c. The back leg is cast downward and the shoulders are pulled over the bar as the body rises in the rear. This motion provides the extra lift which enables the performer to finish in a support position over the bar.

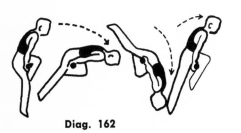

Diag. 162

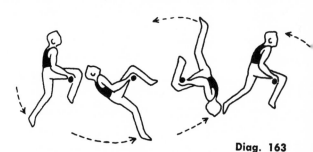

Diag. 163

SPOTTING SUGGESTIONS

Refer to Intermediate Skills, Horizontal Bar No. 3. (Bar should be at chest height when first learning the skill.)

Backward

    a. Perform a single leg circle mount to a support on the bar.

    b. With a regular grip, cast the rear leg backward and hook the knee of the front leg over the bar. Drive the rear leg hard in a circular pattern.

    c. The rear leg is thrown over the bar at the completion of the circle. Finish in a support position.

SPOTTING SUGGESTIONS

The instructor may push the student's shoulders during the circle and grasp his free leg, for stability, at the completion of the circle. (Bar should be at chest height when first learning the skill.)

5. *Short Under-swing Dismount* (2 points) (*Diag. 164*)
   a. Perform a back hip circle mount to a front support.
   b. Drop backwards, keeping the bar close to the legs.
   c. Bring the ankles to the bar as the hips swing forward.
   d. At the peak of the forward swing, shoot the legs forward and release the bar. Straighten the body before landing.

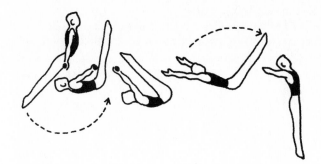

Diag. 164

SPOTTING SUGGESTIONS

Assist the performer by supporting his upper back and guiding him to the mat. Be sure that the arms remain extended throughout the execution of the skill. (Bar should be at chest height when first learning the skill.)

Parallel Bars (suggested value 17 points)

1. *From a Cross Stand at Near End, Single Leg Cut Mount to Lower Arm Support* (2 points) (*Diag. 165*)
   a. Grasp the bars, as illustrated, and jump upward.
   b. Both legs are raised, with one leg cutting over the wrist on the outside of the bar. The other leg follows, but remains between the bars.

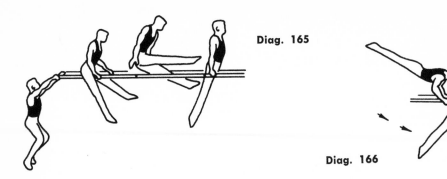

Diag. 165

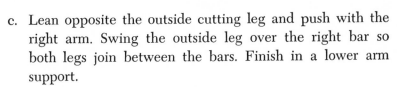

Diag. 166

c. Lean opposite the outside cutting leg and push with the right arm. Swing the outside leg over the right bar so both legs join between the bars. Finish in a lower arm support.

SPOTTING SUGGESTIONS

The instructor may grasp the performer's waist from the rear and guide him into position.

2. *From a Light Swing, Lay Back to Upper Arm Hang and Swing to Piked Position* (2 points) (*Diag. 166*)

a. From a lower arm support position, swing to the rear and drop downward to an upper arm support.

b. Swing body forward and raise the legs to a deep piked position, as illustrated. Hold this position for three seconds.

SPOTTING SUGGESTIONS

The instructor may reach under the bars and grasp the performer's legs with one hand and the abdomen with the other hand as he swings down. Thus, the instructor may control the downward swing. The performer may also be held in the deep piked position by supporting his lower back.

3. *From a Cross Seat, Lower to a Shoulder Balance* (*no hold*) *and Forward Roll to Upper Arm Hang* (2 points) (*Diag. 167*)

a. Assume a straddle seat position.

b. Place hands just in front of legs and lower to the shoulders with elbows pointing out.

c. Tuck the chin into the chest, raise the seat over the head and roll forward supported by upper arms.

d. Finish in an upper arm support position.

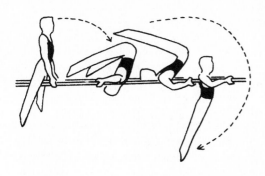

Diag. 167

Spotting Suggestions

Assist by reaching under the bars and supporting the performer's shoulders and lower back. The student's arms (at shoulder) should be in an extended position (in the inverted position) to insure a safe roll.

4. *Five Swinging Dips* (2 points)
   a. Refer to Novice Skills, Parallel Bars No. 3.
5. *From a Cross Stand in Middle of the Bars, Glide Kip to Upper Arm Support* (3 points) (*Diag. 168*)
   a. Jump, with hips raised, and grasp the bars.
   b. Swing and stretch the body forward and downward.
   c. At the end of the swing, bend the hips and bring both legs toward the chest.

Diag. 168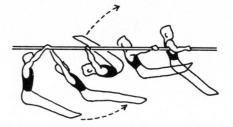

   d. As the body swings backward, a deep piked position is assumed. The legs are then snapped forward and upward along with a vigorous pull of the hands on the bars.
   e. The upper arms are placed over the bars in a support position.

Spot by placing one hand on the student's lower back and the other hand on his "hamstrings" and guide him to the support position.

6. *From a Lower Arm Support Swing to a Reverse Straddle* (2 points) (*Diag. 169*)
   a. From a lower arm support, start a "light" swing.
   b. As the legs start to ascend, in the rear of the swing, straddle the legs (left leg extended and placed over right bar and right leg flexed and placed over left bar) and maintain the grip position on the bars.
   c. When both legs are straddled over the bars, release the grip and complete the half turn.

Diag. 170

Diag. 169

You can reach under the bars and manually assist the student's execution of the straddle. Be sure to have him hold on to the bars until the turn is completed. Place the bars at chest height when first learning the skill.

7. *Front Dismount with a Half Turn to an Even Left Side Stand* (4 points) (*Diag. 170*)
   a. Swing to the rear and place both legs over the left bar.
   b. Release the right bar and execute a half turn to the right.
   c. As the body descends, change the left hand to an overhand grip and land with control.

You may assist by grasping the student's left upper arm and wrist and guiding him through the skill. Bar should be at chest height when first learning this skill.

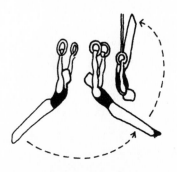

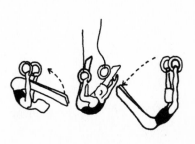

Diag. 171   **Diag. 172**

Still Rings (suggested value 14 points)

1. *From a Hang, Swing to Inverted Hang in Arch Position* (3 points) (*Diag. 171*)
   a. From a hanging position, obtain a swing.
   b. Swing upward, with a strong arm pull, and assume arched hang position, as illustrated.
   c. Return to the starting position.

Assist the pupil by controlling him in the inverted position. Lack of kinesthetic sense will often cause the pupil to over- or under-spin the skill. Be prepared for this situation by controlling his chest and back at all times.

2. *Three Dips from a Support* (2 points)
   a. Refer to Beginner Skills, Parallel Bars No. 1.
3. *From a Piked Inverted Hang, Swing Forward to a Single Leg Cut and Regrasp* (*both feet*) (3 points) (*Diag. 172*)
   a. Swing to a piked inverted hang position.
   b. Rock forward and cut right leg over right wrist while pulling upward with both arms.

c. Regrasp the ring and bring both legs together, as illustrated.

Have the student first practice the "rocking position" with both legs (without regrasping). Then have him cut the single leg. Spot by supporting his upper back.

4. *From a Hang, Swing to an Inlocate* (4 points) (*Diag. 173*)
    a. From a hanging position, cast downward with both legs.
    b. Drive legs upward in the rear.
    c. Spread both rings, tuck chin into the chest and raise the hips.
    d. Continue rolling forward until piked inverted hang position is assumed.

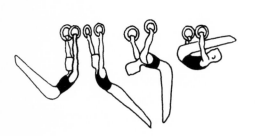

Diag. 173

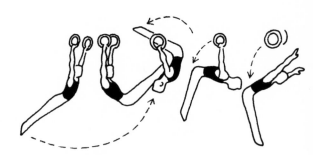

Diag. 174

As the student pikes at the waist, raise his chest with your right hand (to help take some of the strain off his shoulders) and support his neck with your left hand. This will put him into the piked inverted hang position.

5. *From a Hang, Swing to a Back Roll Dismount* (2 points) (*Diag. 174*)
    a. Swing through an open inverted hang position.
    b. As the body passes the rings, the eyes should be focused on the landing area.
    c. Release the rings when legs are in position for landing.

SPOTTING SUGGESTIONS

Refer to Beginner Skills, Horizontal Bar No. 3.

Tumbling (suggested value 9 points)

1. *Two Dive Forward Rolls* (3 points) (*Diag. 175*)
   a. Take off with both feet at a 45° angle.
   b. The body should be in a fully extended position.
   c. Forward rotation is controlled by hip extension. The raising of the legs will lower the torso and put the performer into a vertical position.
   d. Tuck the head and support the landing with both hands and go into a roll.

Diag. 175

Diag. 176

SPOTTING SUGGESTIONS

Refer to Beginner Skills, Tumbling No. 2.
2. *Handspring Off Rolled Mat* (2 points) (*Diag. 176*)
   a. Step and hurdle (Novice Skills, Tumbling No. 5a).
   b. Kick through a handstand position on the rolled mats.
   c. Arch the back and push out in the shoulders, with extended arms, as the body overbalances.
   d. Stand with head up, and arms extended over head with back slightly arched.

SPOTTING SUGGESTIONS

The instructor should hold the performer's upper arm and lower back as he passes through the handstand position. Assist the student by sitting on the rolled mat (straddle seat to either side) and grasping his wrist and by supporting his upper back. Follow him through the skill until he maintains an upright position.

3. *Dive to Three-point Balance and Forward Roll* (2 points) (*Diag. 177*)

    a. From a semi-squat position execute a slight dive in piked position.

Diag. 177

    b. When contact with the mat is made the body weight should be equally divided on both hands and the head (especially in the forehead area—piked head balance).

    c. Maintain hand contact with the mat until the torso passes the vertical position and then go into the forward roll. This is an excellent lead up to the headspring.

SPOTTING SUGGESTIONS

When the student dives to the three-point balance, control him by supporting the torso. Make sure that he passes the vertical position before going into the roll.

4. *Back Extension* (2 points) (*Diag. 178*)

    a. From a standing position, sit backward and shoot legs upward to a near handstand.

Diag. 178

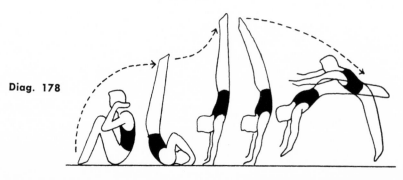

b. Snap legs downward to a stand (*see* Intermediate Skills, Free Calisthenics No. 2).

Since most students find it difficult to go to the near handstand position, it is advisable that you support the student's legs as he opens out of the piked position. Early tendencies are to either over- or under- shoot the skill.

Rope Climb (suggested value 5 points)

1. *Climb 20 Feet with Feet and Hands* (4 points)
   a. Refer to Beginner Skills, Rope Climb No. 1.

Junior

Skills

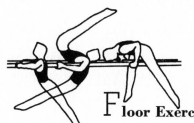

VIII

F**loor Exercise** (suggested value 21 points)

1. *Keep Beat to 3/4 and 2/4 Time* (1 point)
2. *Three Leaps Across Floor* (1 point) (*Diag. 179*)
   a. Take two steps and leap upward with a vigorous throw of one leg and both arms.

    b. The head and chest are held high and the legs are in maximum split position. Upon landing, step and leap again until three consecutive leaps have been performed. The position of the body is important, as well as the height and form that is demonstrated.

3. *Shoulder Support with Hands on Hips* (1 point) (*Diag. 180*)
    a. From a sitting position, roll backward and extend the hips.
    b. Rest the elbows and upper arms on the floor while grasping the hips. Hold this position, as illustrated, for three seconds.

Diag. 179   **Diag. 180**   **Diag. 181**   **Diag. 182**

SPOTTING SUGGESTIONS

    Stand to the rear of the student and place your knee against the pupil's buttocks. Offer support until the fully extended position is maintained.

4. *Two or Three Running Steps and Hitch Kick* (1 point) (*Diag. 181*)
    a. Take two steps and kick the left leg upward.
    b. As the left leg descends, the right leg is kicked in the same manner. Both legs switch in the air and the left leg lands as the right leg remains in the high position.

5. *From Standing Position, Lower to Back Bend* (1 point) (*Diag. 182*)
    a. From a standing position, with feet about shoulder-width apart, slowly lean backward.

b. Bend both knees and push the hips forward as the upper body drops lower to the floor. Both arms are extended and elevated overhead reaching for the floor.

c. Place hands on the floor and hold for three seconds.

SPOTTING SUGGESTIONS

As the student starts the maneuver, support his lower back until the four-point support is maintained.

6. *From Standing Position, Jump to Arch Position* (1 point) (*Diag. 183*)

   a. From a stand, jump to hyper-extended arch position, with both arms overhead.

   b. Land with hips in semi-flexed position.

7. *From Standing Position, Fall to Bent Arm Front Support, One Leg Hyper-extended* (2 points) (*Diag. 184*)

   a. From a stand, fall forward placing hands on mat, with one leg extended upward, as illustrated. Hold for three seconds.

Diag. 184

Diag. 185

Diag. 183

SPOTTING SUGGESTIONS

Have a student practice on mat to take the strain off the wrists.

8. *From Front Support, Snap to Pike, Arched Pike Stand* (2 points) (*Diag. 185*)

   a. Execute a front support position.

b. Snap hips upward to a semi-piked position, while pushing away from the floor.

c. Arch back to a hyper-extended position and snap the legs close to the hands on the floor. At the same moment, push vigorously with the hands trying to raise the hands high off the floor before landing.

9. *From Front Support, Cut Both Legs Under Either Arm to Back Support in Arch Position* (2 points) (*Diag. 186*)

a. Assume front support position.

b. Snap hips upward by pushing with toes.

c. Pick up left arm, lean to the right, and swing both legs around the left side of body. Replace the left arm.

d. Assume a rear support position.

Diag. 186

Diag. 187

SPOTTING SUGGESTIONS

Have the student practice on a mat to take the strain off the wrists.

10. *Head Balance to a Forward Roll Straddle Stand* (2 points) (*Diag. 187*)

a. Assume a headstand position as described in Intermediate Skills, Floor Exercise No. 1.

b. Flex the neck and roll forward while straddling the legs as wide as possible and place both hands between the legs.

c. When hands make contact with the floor, push until a straddle balance is assumed. Raise both arms, as illustrated, and hold for three seconds.

11. *From a Sitting Position: lay back to back extension and snap-down with one leg and half turn to stand with free leg in a forward piked position* (2 points) *(Diag. 188)*

   a. Perform a back extension roll, as described in Intermediate Skills, Tumbling No. 5.

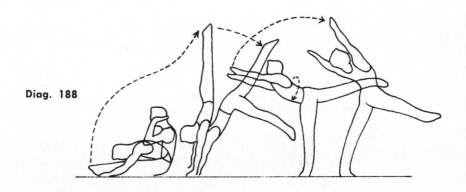

Diag. 188

   b. Lower the left leg, placing the foot as close to the hands as possible.

   c. Assume a scale position (Novice Skills, Free Calisthenics No. 6) momentarily.

   d. Perform a half turn to the right and step forward.

12. *From Front Support, Straddle Both Legs Under Arms to a Rear Support* (2 points) *(Diag. 189)*

   a. Assume front support position.

Diag. 189

   b. Snap hips upward by pushing with toes.

   c. Straddle legs as wide as possible and push off the floor with both hands. Pass legs under hands and assume a rear support position. Hold for three seconds.

Diag. 190

Have the student practice on a mat to take the strain off the wrists.

13. *Two Cartwheels to Quarter Turn and Immediate Handstand (no hold) and Forward Roll to Stand* (4 points) (*Diag. 190*)
    a. Refer to Intermediate Skills, Floor Exercise Nos. 5a and b.
    b. Include an additional cartwheel.

Long Horse (suggested value 7 points)

Horse in Cross Position at Standard Height

1. *Straddle Vault from the Croup* (3 points) (*Diag. 191*)
    a. The take-off from the beat board should be forceful enough to carry the body over the length of the horse.
    b. When contact with the croup is made, you should push vigorously with the hands and maintain a slight piked position.
    c. Straddle the legs and pass vertically over the horse with the arms raised overhead and the body completely stretched.

Diag. 191

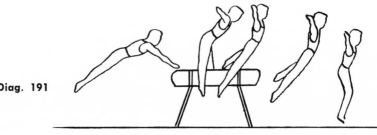

122

SPOTTING SUGGESTIONS

As the student makes contact with the croup, follow him along the horse and be ready to assist, by supporting his lower back, in the event he does not clear the neck of the horse or if he under-balances during the flight.

2. *Squat Vault from the Croup* (4 points) (*Diag. 192*)
   a. Run fast with a good forward lean. The beat board should be placed back further than usual because the hand placement on the horse is at the croup.
   b. Dive forward and reach for the croup with the arms extended; the eyes should be focused on the croup.
   c. Push off vigorously with both hands, and bring the knees into the chest.
   d. Straighten the body as the legs clear the neck of the horse.

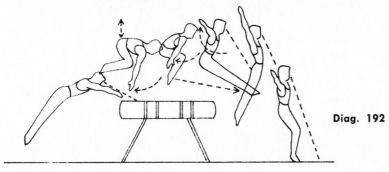

Diag. 192

SPOTTING SUGGESTIONS

Spot by standing in front of the neck of the horse. As the student vaults, move in and be prepared to support his chest in the event he catches his feet on the neck or if he should over-spin the skill. Often the boy will open or arch out too soon and this action might possibly cause him to under-spin the skill; in this event support his upper back.

Side Horse (suggested value 17 points)

1. *From an Even Front Stand with Left Hand on the Right Pommel (regular outer grip) and Right Hand on the Croup:*

jump to a front support and cut right leg under right hand, immediately straddle half turn to right, pivoting on the left arm, to straddle support over the right pommel; continue to swing the right leg over the left pommel and under the right hand, slight travel to right and join legs to front support over the saddle (3 points) (*Diag. 193*)

a. Assume a front support position over the croup of the horse.

b. Swing the right leg forward under the right hand. Replace the right hand on the end and swing the left leg over the saddle.

c. Push with the right hand, swing the right leg to the rear and execute a half turn to the right to a straddle support over the right pommel. (The right hand may be replaced, for added push, after the right leg has been brought to the rear.)

d. Swing the right leg to the rear over the neck and immediately swing the left leg to the rear over the croup and slight travel to the right and to a front support.

Diag. 193

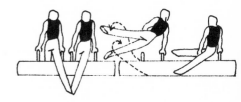

Diag. 194

SPOTTING SUGGESTIONS

Stand to the front of the student (even position) and be ready to steady him by supporting his waist should he lose his balance, especially during the execution of positions two, three and four.

2. *From Straddle Support Over the Saddle, Execute One Reverse Scissor to Either Side* (1 point) (*Diag. 194*)

a. Assume a straddle support position over the saddle.

b. Swing both legs up to the right, then back to the left.

c. Lean to the right, push off the left pommel with the left hand, and switch both legs. The front leg always goes over the rear leg as both legs exchange positions.

d. Assume a straddle support position in the saddle.

Have the student practice this move with long trousers to avoid leg abrasions.

3. *From Straddle Support Over the Saddle Execute a Regular Scissor, Both Right and Left* (2 points) (*Diag. 195*)

a. Refer to Intermediate Skills, Side Horse No. 2.

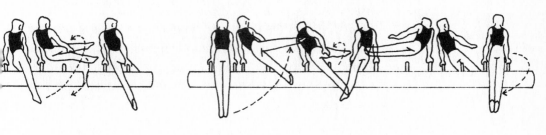

Diag. 195   **(left to right)**   **Diag. 196**

Refer to Junior Skills, Side Horse No. 2.

4. *From Front Support Over the Saddle: swing the right leg under the right hand and over the right pommel and continue swinging under left hand and over left pommel to a front support, continue swinging right leg over right pommel (single leg full circle with stationary leg in rear) and immediate regular scissor to the left* (3 points)

a. Refer to Intermediate Skills, Side Horse No. 5.

b. Once in the front support position, continue swinging right leg over right pommel to a regular scissor left (refer to Junior Skills, Side Horse No. 3).

5. *From Front Support Over the Saddle: swing the right leg over the right pommel and swing the left leg over the left pommel*

and immediately pick up both legs to half double leg circle to front support (3 points) (*Diag. 196*)

a. Assume front support position.

b. Swing right leg under right hand and left leg under left hand to a rear support.

c. Join both legs in front and immediately swing them under the right hand to a front support.

SPOTTING SUGGESTIONS

After the legs are joined in the rear support position, have the student fully extend the hips, as well as keep the buttocks away from the horse (figure 6). This procedure will alleviate the difficulty of maintaining the front support position (figure 7).

6. *From Rear Support Over Saddle: under-cut with the left leg to a straddle support and continue swinging to the left to a rear support. Repeat three times* (2 points) (*Diag. 197*)

a. Extend the hips. Lean to the left and under-cut the left leg to straddle support.

Diag. 197

b. Lean to the right and continue swinging left leg to the left to a rear support.

c. Repeat three times.

SPOTTING SUGGESTIONS

Support the student's hips as he attempts the initial under-cut. In doing so, give him a little support to assist him in executing the skill.

7. *From Front Support Over the Croup: feint with the left leg and execute three-quarter double leg circle to a flank dismount*

with a quarter turn left to an even right side stand (3 points)
(*Diag. 198*)

Diag. 198

a. Assume a front support position over the croup.
b. Feint with the left leg over the left wrist.
c. Swing the left leg to the rear, join both legs and execute a three-quarter double leg circle (refer to Junior Skills, Side Horse No. 5—Spotting Suggestions)
d. Lean to the right and flank the body over the croup with a quarter turn to left to a cross right side stand.

SPOTTING SUGGESTIONS

Refer to Intermediate Skills, Side Horse, No. 6.

Horizontal Bar (suggested value 14 points)

1. *From a Hang Cast and Kip Up to a Front Support* (4 points)
   (*Diag. 199*)
   a. Jump to hang and cast to a small underswing.
   b. At the *peak* of the forward swing, flex the hips and touch the toes to the bar.
   c. After completing *b*, and without pause, extend the hips while shooting both legs upward along the bar, and pull simultaneously downward into the abdomen.

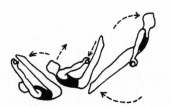

Diag. 199

Spotting Suggestions

Assist the performer by supporting his lower back with one hand and his upper legs with the other. As the performer swings backward, help him to arrive at a supportive position.

2. *From Rear Support, One Full Backward Circle* (2 points) (*Diag. 200*)
    a. Assume rear support position.
    b. Push hips backward (flexion) and hook knees over the bar.
    c. Drop the head backward and circle back to a rear support position.

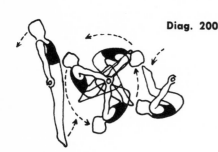

Diag. 200

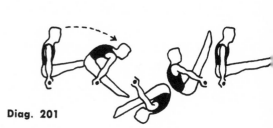

Diag. 201

Spotting Suggestions

Spot by placing your right hand (supinated) on the student's chest to help him complete the circular motion and with the left hand secure his grip on the bar by applying pressure on his lower legs. To insure a maximum knee grip, the pupil's feet should be in dorsiflexion (bar at chest height).

3. *From Front Support, Forward Hip Circle to a Front Support* (2 points)
    The bar should be at chest height when first learning the skill.
    Refer to Advanced Skills, Horizontal Bar No. 3.

4. *From Rear Support, Swing to a Forward Seat Circle* (2 points) (*Diag. 201*)
    a. Assume a sitting position on the bar with a double under grip.

b. Raise the hips and place the bar behind the knees without touching your legs to the bar. Lean forward, maintaining flexed position.

c. Perform one complete circle forward.

SPOTTING SUGGESTIONS

This skill should be practiced on a low bar so that you will be able to guide the student into the correct positions. Spot by standing to the side of the student and behind his right arm. Reach under the bar and grasp his right wrist, with an outer grip. As he falls into the move, reach under with your left hand, while supporting his wrist, and control his upper back throughout the maneuver. Bar should be at shoulder height when first learning the skill.

5. *From Front Support, Execute a Flank Dismount to an Even Rear Stand* (2 points) (*Diag. 202*)

    a. Assume a front support position.
    b. Cast backward, away from the bar, maintaining straight arm support.
    c. Raise hips, in flexed position, and lean to the right while swinging both legs over the bar on the left side.

Diag. 202

d. Extend the hips while passing over the bar. Push off the bar and dismount to an even rear stand.

SPOTTING SUGGESTIONS

Spot by grasping the performer's supporting arm and guide him over the bar to a safe landing. Bar should be at shoulder height when first learning the skill.

6. *Cast and in Back Swing Place the Hands Together, and in Forward Swing Engage the Legs on the Bar and Release Hands and Swing Forward to Dismount* (2 points) (*Diag. 203*)

    a. From a hanging position below the bar, cast and obtain a medium swing; on the back swing place hands together, at the peak of the forward swing, straddle both legs and hook them over the bar.

    b. At the peak of the backward swing, disengage both hands from the bar and straighten the body, as illustrated. As the hands are removed from the bar, they are cast over the head and downward.

Diag. 203

    c. Keep the knees hooked until the peak of the knee circle is reached. Straighten the knees and focus the eyes on the landing area for the dismount.

Spotting Suggestions

Assist by grasping the performer's arm as he circles the bar, and guide him to the mat. It is also advisable to keep the feet in dorsiflexion to insure a stronger knee grip on the bar.

Parallel Bars (suggested value 15 points)

1. *From an Even Front Stand with a Mixed Grip on Near Bar, Flank Mount and Quarter Turn to Lower Arm Support* (2 points) (*Diag. 204*)

a. Stand facing the bars with hands in a mixed grip or double over-grip.

b. Jump upward, while pushing down with the arms and raising the hips.

c. Continue pushing downward until the hips are well above the bars. Disengage both hands and rear vault over the near bar, as illustrated. Assume a lower arm support position as quickly as possible.

Diag. 204

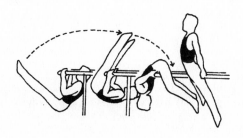

Diag. 205

Spotting Suggestions

Spot by standing to the right side of the student. As he executes the stunt, be prepared to support his upper back, should he fall backward, or assist by reaching under the bars, with both arms, should he miss his lower arm support. The bar should be at chest height when first learning; the beat board can be used for additional elevation of the pupil.

2. *From a Cross Stand at Far End, Straddle Mount Backward to a Cross Straddle Seat* (2 points) (*Diag. 205*)

a. Grasp the ends of the bars, as illustrated, and roll over backwards, in a piked position, with both arms flexed.

b. Continue pulling with the arms as the body turns over.

c. Straddle both bars and change the hand position to an over bar grip. Practice changing the grip rapidly.

d. Assume a straddle position as illustrated.

Spot by standing to the side of the student; grasp his left wrist with your right hand, outer grip; and with your left hand support his left shoulder as he begins the maneuver.

3. *From an Even Right Side Stand with a Mixed Grip, Under Bar Pivot Mount to an Upper Arm Hang* (1 point) *(Diag. 206)*
   a. Grasp the near bar with a mixed grip.
   b. Raise both legs into a piked position, on the outside of the bars, and swing under the bars with a half turn to the left.

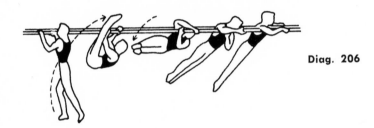

Diag. 206

   c. The right upper arm is pulled over the bar as the legs fall downward. An upper arm hang position is assumed.

Assist by supporting the performer's abdomen and hips at the completion of the turn.

4. *From a Cross Lower Arm Support, Execute a Single Leg Cut in Back Swing Over One Bar to Lower Arm Support (both legs)* (1 point) *(Diag. 207)*
   a. Take a small swing to the rear in a lower arm support.

Diag. 207
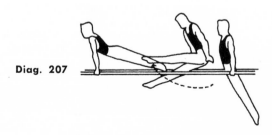

b. Lean to the right, push with the left hand and swing the left leg over the left bar. The right leg follows the left leg between the bars.

c. Both legs join on the front swing.

Spotting Suggestions

Use the low bars and assist by grasping the performer's right upper arm to keep him from falling between the bars.

5. *From an Upper Arm Hang, Swing and Three-quarter Back Roll to a Straddle Support* (2 points) (*Diag. 208*)

a. Obtain a strong swing in an upper arm hang position.

b. Swing to a deep piked position, as illustrated.

c. Roll over backwards, on upper arms, and straddle the legs.

d. While rotating on the shoulders, reach backward with both hands and grasp the bars. Assume a straddle support position.

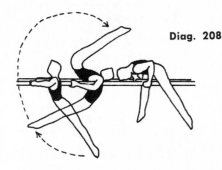

Diag. 208

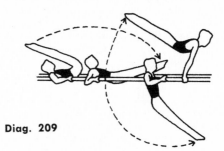

Diag. 209

Spotting Suggestions

Assist by reaching below the bars and support the performer's lower back and shoulders as he rolls over backward. You can also reach under and give support to the abdominal area to insure a safe landing during the early stages of learning.

6. *From an Upper Arm Hang, Hips in Piked Position, Back Up-Rise* (2 points) (*Diag. 209*)

a. Swing to a deep piked position, as illustrated.

b. Cast legs forward to a straight body position.

c. As the body passes below the bars, a slightly piked position is assumed.

d. Drive the heels upward, by hyper-extending the lower back, push down with the hands to full arm extension and lean forward as the body rises in the rear.

e. Assume a lower arm support.

SPOTTING SUGGESTIONS

The instructor may assist the student by reaching below the bars and pushing against the student's chest as he rises in the upward position.

7. *From Straddle Seat, Lower to a Cross Shoulder Balance and Hold for Three Seconds* (3 points) (*Diag. 210*)

a. Assume a straddle support position.

b. Place the hands just in front of the thighs, lower the upper arms to the bars with the *elbows out* and raise the hips over the head by flexing the hips.

c. Slowly extend the hips and raise the legs over the head to the balanced position. Hold for three seconds and return to the starting position.

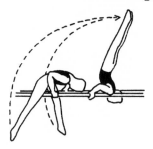

Diag. 210

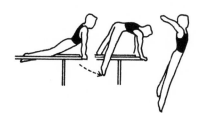

Diag. 211

SPOTTING SUGGESTIONS

Aid the student throughout the movement by helping him to raise his legs and by supporting his shoulders.

8. *From a Lower Arm Support, at Far End, Swing and Straddle Off to a Cross Rear Stand* (2 points) (*Diag. 211*)

a. Obtain a slight swing from a lower arm support at the end of the bars.

b. At the rear of the swing, flex the hips, push with both arms and straddle both legs over the bars.

c. Straighten the body in the air before landing.

Assist by standing directly in front of the performer; support him after straddling by grasping him under the upper arms. Place bar at chest level when first learning this skill.

Still Rings (suggested value 15 points)

1. *With a False Grip Execute a Muscle-up* (3 points) (*Diag. 212*)
   a. From a hang, obtain a false grip by reaching over the ring so that the wrist and the heel of the hand are in contact with the ring. The wrist is flexed as much as possible.
   b. Pull upwards until the bottom of the ring is at chest level.

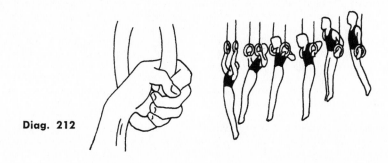

Diag. 212

c. Turn the wrists outward and push downward as if dipping on the parallel bars. The pull-up and push-up action should be continuous.

Assist the performer by lifting him into position for the "muscle up."

2. *From a Support, Lean Forward and Drop to a Piked Position* (1 point) (*Diag. 213*)
   a. Assume lower arm support position.

b. Turn the wrists outward and roll forward to piked inverted hang position. This trick should be performed slowly and with control.

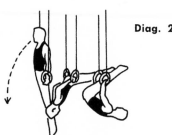

Diag. 213

Diag. 214

SPOTTING SUGGESTIONS

You should carefully spot this move because too sudden a drop might possibly cause the student to lose his grip. As the pupil rolls forward, place your left hand on his abdomen (standing at his side) and your right hand behind his neck. If the height of the rings do not permit your placing one hand on his chest, move in directly to his neck and upper back.

3. *From a Support Lean Backward and Drop to Piked Position* (1 point) (*Diag. 214*)
    a. Assume a lower arm support position.
    b. Turn wrists inward and roll backward to piked inverted hang position.

SPOTTING SUGGESTIONS

Stand to the side of the pupil, as he rolls backward, place your left hand on his upper back; when the piked inverted position is established, place your right hand on his chest and guide him to a safe landing.

4. *From Piked Position Cast to a Back Up-rise* (4 points) (*Diag. 215*)
    a. Assume a piked inverted hang position.

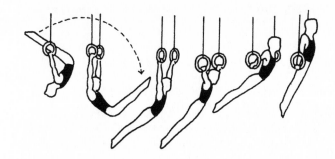

Diag. 215

b. Cast legs upward and pull up with the arms. Extend the hips as the body swings downward.

c. Drive the heels upward, by hyper-extending the hips, at the rear of the swing, and pull downward on the rings.

d. Continue pulling on the rings until the arms are in a horizontal position, then push vigorously; a support position is assumed.

SPOTTING SUGGESTIONS

Assist by standing to one side of the student and pushing his legs upward at the rear of the swing. The student should be told to keep the rings close to his hips and slightly forward in the early stages of learning this skill. This procedure will counteract the center of gravity from being moved too far forward and thus stabilize the student in the supportive position. In the event the pupil does fall forward, support him on the chest or if the situation calls for it, grasp him around the waist with both arms.

5. *From a Piked Position Dislocate* (4 points) (*Diag. 216*)
    a. Assume a piked inverted hang position.
    b. Pull with the arms and shoot the legs backward well above a horizontal plane.

Diag. 216

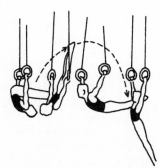

c. Turn the wrists outward and extend the arms outward away from the body. Place the rings forward in front of the body as the legs descend.

SPOTTING SUGGESTIONS

The student *must* be spotted during his early attempts at performing a dislocate. You should slowly move the student through the correct positions before he is ever allowed to solo the dislocate.

Standing to the side of the performer, place your left hand, palm in supination, on his chest (move into this position by going in from the bicep portion of the arm) and your right hand on his thighs. As the dislocate is executed, lift the student's chest with the left hand and support his legs with the right hand. Care should be taken not to let him hit "bottom" too severely. This sudden jerk on the arms might possibly cause him to lose his grip.

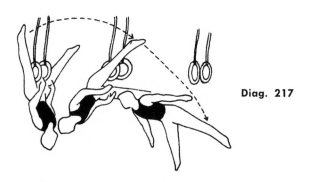

Diag. 217

6. *Cast and Back Double Leg Cut-off* (2 points) (*Diag. 217*)
   a. Assume a piked inverted hang position.
   b. Cast and swing to the rear.
   c. Swing forward and straddle legs.
   d. Straddle legs over wrists and release the rings.
   e. Bring legs together and land.

SPOTTING SUGGESTIONS

Due to the student's ascent during this skill, your hands have to be in the ready position in the event of a mishap. As the student goes for the straddle, your left hand should be in a straight plane with his chest; this will serve as a check for under-rotation. As the straddle nears completion, your right hand should move into a straight plane with the upper back; this will serve as a check for over-rotation.

Tumbling (suggested value 8 points)

1. *Headspring* (2 points) (*Diag. 218*)
   a. Assume a squat position.
   b. Roll forward and place head on the floor, as illustrated.

(left to right) Diag. 218

   c. Shoot legs upward by extending the hips and push with both arms.
   d. Continue pushing with the arms and arch the back to a hyper-extended position.
   e. Reach backward under the body with both feet and stand.

SPOTTING SUGGESTIONS

Assist by supporting the performer's upper back and by guiding him to his feet.

2. *Front Handspring* (2 points) (*Diag. 219*)
   a. Step and hurdle with arms over head.
   b. Place hands close to the forward leg and kick through a handstand position.

Diag. 219

    c. Elevate the shoulders, extend the hips and place the feet under the body to a stand.

SPOTTING SUGGESTIONS

Refer to Intermediate Skills, Tumbling No. 2.

3. *Back Handspring* (4 points) (*Diag. 220*)
    a. Assume a semi-squat position, as illustrated.
    b. Lean backward, as though sitting in a chair, and swing arms backward while pushing with the legs.
    c. Arch the back and reach with both arms to an elevated position.

Diag. 220

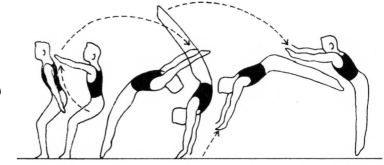

    d. Place the hands on the mat, about shoulder width apart, and snap the legs downward.
    e. Stand with arms stretched forward.

SPOTTING SUGGESTIONS

The skill *must* be spotted in the early learning stages. To give the student a "feeling of sureness," kneel down at his side and place your raised leg beneath the pupil's buttocks while resting your forearm (in supine position) on your upper thigh. Have the student lean back and put him through the skill.

After the student gets the "feel" of this maneuver, stand behind him while placing one hand around his neck; then have him jump upward to an arched position. This will introduce him to the second part of the skill. Next, stand or kneel by his side and have him execute the handspring. It might be advisable to have an assistant helping to spot on the performer's other side during the beginning stages of learning.

Rope Climb (suggested value 3 points)

1. *Climb 15 feet Without Using Legs*
   a. From a standing position, climb hand over hand to the 15-foot mark without using legs. The rope should be placed between the legs for the duration of the climb.

Advanced

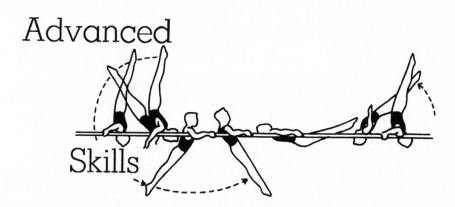

Skills

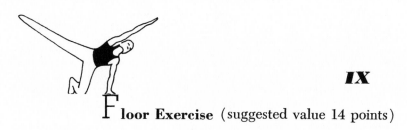

IX

Floor Exercise (suggested value 14 points)

1. *Front Handspring to Headspring (3 points) (Diag. 221)*
   a. This is a combination of two skills that have been described and illustrated in previous lessons.
   b. Refer to Junior Skills, Tumbling Nos. 1 and 2.

Diag. 221

2. *From a Stand, Step Forward with Either Leg to Immediate Jump with Half Turn to Scale* (2 points) (*Diag. 222*)
   a. Step forward with the left foot and kick the right leg upward. Both arms are raised sideward as the hip is flexed.
   b. Perform a half turn with the upper body, maintaining a vertical position, and land on the left foot.

Diag. 222

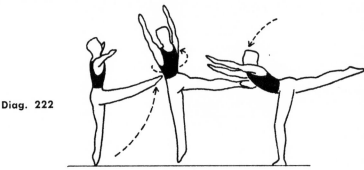

   c. Lower the upper body, and raise the right leg to a scale position. Hold for three seconds.

SPOTTING´ SUGGESTIONS

As the half turn is performed, have the student land on a slightly flexed knee and then extend it to the scale position. This procedure will eliminate unnecessary sprains to the knee joint.

3. *From Prone Position with Arms Extended Forward, Pull Forward and Press, with Straight Legs, to a Head Balance (2 points) (Diag. 223)*
   a. Assume a front support with arms elevated in front of body, as illustrated.
   b. Pull forward with hands, and place head on the floor.
   c. Slowly raise hips, and assume headstand position.

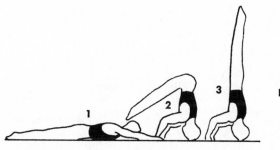

Diag. 223

SPOTTING SUGGESTIONS

Refer to Intermediate Skills, Free Calisthenics No. 1.

4. *Kick to Handstand and Hold for Three Seconds (2 points)*
   a. Refer to Novice Skills, Floor Exercises No. 8.
5. *From Standing Position, Sit with Straight Legs to a back extension and immediately snap-down to a back handspring (2 points) (Diag. 224)*

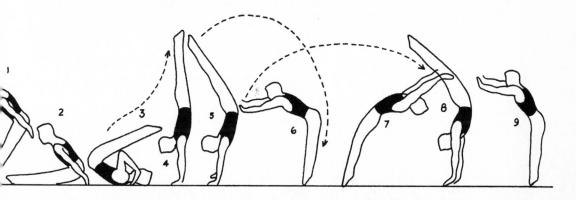

Diag. 224

a. This is a combination of two skills that have been described and illustrated in previous lessons. Refer to Intermediate Skills, Tumbling No. 5 and Junior Skills, Tumbling No. 3. The Nos. 5 and 6 positions—the snap-down—should be referred to in Intermediate Skills, Free Calisthenics, No. 2.

6. *Snap-down to a Back Handspring, Half Turn to Immediate Front Handspring* (3 points) (*Diag. 225*)

Diag. 225

a. This is a combination of tricks that have been described and illustrated in earlier lessons. Refer to Intermediate Skills, Free Calisthenics No. 2, and Junior Skills, Tumbling, Nos. 2 and 3.

Long Horse (suggested value 9 points)

Horse in Cross Position (standard height)

1. *Bent Arm Handspring from Neck* (3.5 points) (*Diag. 226*)
   a. From a fast run, jump upward and outward with the lower back in an arched position.

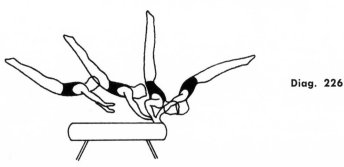

Diag. 226

b. As the hands contact the neck, the body should be in a three-quarter handstand position (30 degrees environ).
c. Flex the arms and lean forward as the feet pass overhead.
d. Once overbalanced, extend the arms and push away for the landing.

SPOTTING SUGGESTIONS

Spot by standing to the side of the performer and place one hand on his upper arm and the other hand on his lower back. With this method of spotting, you will place the student on his feet and guide him through the vault.

2. *Sheep Vault* (5.5 points) (*Diag. 227*)
   a. From a fast run, jump forward with both arms elevated in front of the body.
   b. Push-off the neck and flex the hips.

Diag. 227

c. Arch the back, raise the head, flex the knees and extend the arms sideward, as illustrated. Extend the knees before landing.

SPOTTING SUGGESTIONS

Assist by standing in front of the performer and by supporting him under the upper arms as he lands.

Side Horse (suggested value 14 points)

1. *From an Even Front Stand, with Left Hand on Neck and Right Hand on Left Pommel: flank vault mount with half turn*

right and continue swinging left leg over saddle and grasping left hand to left pommel to front straddle support (3 points) (*Diag. 228*)

a. Assume an even front stand, as illustrated.

b. Jump to a flank over the neck of the horse, keeping the hips close to the right hand. The right arm remains extended throughout this maneuver.

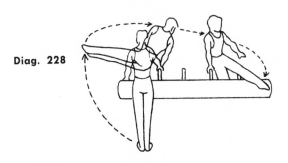

Diag. 228

c. Complete a half turn while pivoting on the right hand and swing the left leg over the horse, left hand should grasp right pommel at skills completion, as illustrated. Finish in a front straddle support.

SPOTTING SUGGESTIONS

You should assist the student during this maneuver; do so by standing at his right side. Place your right hand on his right wrist and your left hand on his triceps. As the student executes the mount, support his arm while guiding him through the skill. To avoid his path of movement, move to your left as he nears completion of the skill.

2. *From an Even Straddle Support Over Saddle, Execute a Reverse Scissor on Both Sides* (3 points) (*Diag. 229*)

a. Refer to Junior Skills, Side Horse No. 2.

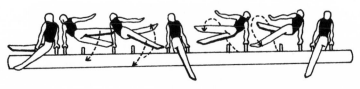

Diag. 229

3. *From a Rear Support Over Croup or Neck, Execute a Single Leg Full Circle with Stationary Leg in Front and Back (2 points) (Diags. 230-231)*

Stationary Leg in Front
  a. Assume a rear support position on neck, and swing right leg over pommel to the rear.

Diag. 230

  b. Continue swinging right leg around until rear support position is assumed once again.

Stationary Leg in Back
  a. These movements are variations of the single leg circles described in earlier lessons (Intermediate Skills, Side Horse No. 5).
  b. From a front support on neck, swing right leg under left leg and over the end of the horse.
  c. Continue swinging leg around until front support position is assumed.

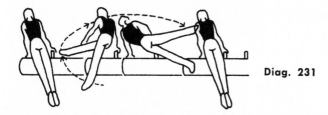

Diag. 231

4. *From a Front Support Over Saddle, Feint with Either Leg to a Double Rear Vault Dismount to an Even Left Side Stand (3 points) (Diag. 232)*

Diag. 232

(left to right)

a. Assume feint position, as illustrated.
b. Swing the right leg rearward and join both legs in the rear and swing them over the left pommel. The right arm remains straight and the legs are held high.
c. Both legs pass over the croup as the left hand reaches for the croup and the dismount is completed.

SPOTTING SUGGESTIONS

You can assist the student by standing to his rear, just opposite his right arm (stand far enough to his rear so as not to interfere with the feint motion). As his right leg swings around past the right arm supportive position (figure 4), move in and support his right wrist with your left hand and his right tricep with your right hand. Guide him throughout the exercise.

5. *With Left Hand on the Neck and Right Hand on the Left Pommel, Jump to a Cross Front Rest and Continue Swinging Legs Over Pommel to a Cross Side Stand (loop off) (3 points) (Diag. 233)*
    a. With right hand on the left pommel and left hand on neck, jump to cross front support and continue swinging legs

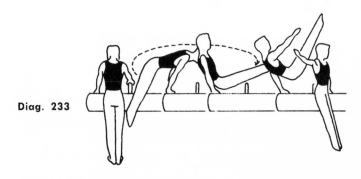

Diag. 233

over pommel, (this involves the temporary release of the left hand on the neck) by a quick rotary motion of the hips.

b. Continue pushing vigorously with both hands while flexing the hips.

c. Release the right hand and land in an even left side stand.

Have the student practice jumping to the cross front support. Once this is attained have him stand in a cross front stand and practice the rear vault, then have him put the entire move together. Spot by standing in a cross front stand. As he passes over the neck (figure 3) move in and support his upper back throughout the skill.

Horizontal Bar (suggested value 22 points)

1. *From a Hang, Cast to a Back Up-rise to Immediate Back Hip Circle to a Front Support* (3 points) (*Diag. 234*)
   a. With a regular grip, execute a large cast and swing to the rear.

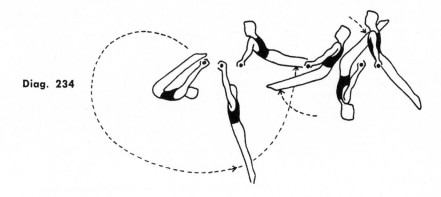

Diag. 234

b. At the peak of the back swing, pull the hips to the bar and assume a slightly piked position.

c. Roll backward around the bar to a front support.

Because this trick requires a high horizontal bar, close spotting is limited. However, by standing just to the side of the performer, you may assist by applying pressure with your hand on the student's chest as he ascends. Once he completes the back circle, stabilize his legs.

2. *From a Front Support, Drop Kip to a Front Support* (2 points) (*Diag. 235*)
   a. Assume front support position.
   b. Drop backward and bring the instep to the bar as the hips swing forward.

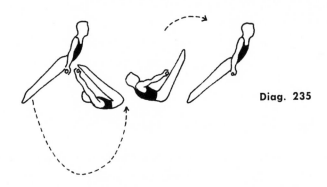

Diag. 235

   c. As the hips swing backward, "shoot" the legs upward by extending the hips, press down on the bar by forcibly extending the shoulder, and secure the bar at the lower abdomen. Assume a front support position.

SPOTTING SUGGESTIONS

Refer to Junior Skills, Horizontal Bar No. 1.

3. *From a Hang, Cast to a Kip Up to Immediate Front Hip Circle to Front Support* (4 points) (*Diag. 236*)
   a. Cast and perform a kip to front support (refer to Junior Skills, Horizontal Bar No. 1).

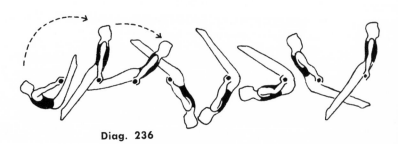

Diag. 236

b. Roll forward with a straight body and break into a tight piked position at the bottom of the swing. Extend the hips and pull the shoulders over the bar and assume front support position.

Spotting Suggestions

This skill can be easily spotted by having the student practice it on the low bar. As he assumes the tight piked position (figure 6), place your left hand on his upper back and your right hand on his thighs. Lift his back and depress his thighs, keeping the bar close to his abdomen.

4. *From a Hang, Cast to a Front Up-rise* (2 points) (*Diag. 237*)
    a. Cast to a moderate swing.
    b. When hips ascend to their maximum height in the front, flex the hip and pass the legs under the bar (this can be accomplished with either straight or flexed knees).
    c. As the hips start to descend from the forward swing, pull vigorously with the arms, keep the neck in a semi-flexed position and maintain the piked position.

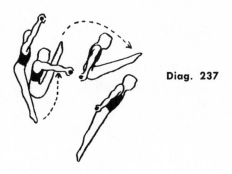

Diag. 237

d. End in an even piked support after shooting legs between the arms.

Spotting Suggestions

As the student starts to "shoot" over the bar, give him support from under the thighs and lower back. Be alert for a loss of balance which might cause the boy to fall backward.

5. *From a Front Support, Cast to Three-quarters Back Giant Swing to a Back Hip Circle to a Front Support* (4 points) (*Diag. 238*)

   a. Assume a front support position with double over-grip.

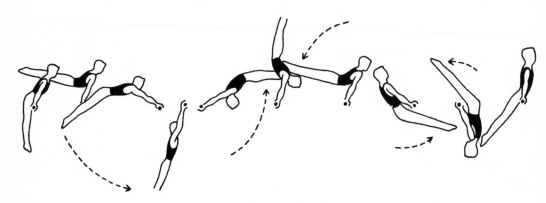

Diag. 238

   b. Cast backward away from the bar and assume a straight body position.
   c. Swing forward until body is approximately horizontal to the floor.
   d. Extend the neck and lower the hips to the bar with straight arms by pivoting on the shoulder joint.
   e. Perform a backward hip circle to a front support.

Spotting Suggestions

Spot by standing to the side of the student. As he passes the median line, apply pressure on his lower back to help guide him through the maneuver. As he lowers his hips to the bar, you can support his legs to avoid his losing control of body momentum.

6. *From a Front Support, Cast to Three-quarters Front Giant Swing and Drop Off to a Front Even Stand* (3 points) (*Diag. 239*)

   a. Assume a front support position with double under-grip.
   b. Cast legs over head through a handstand position.

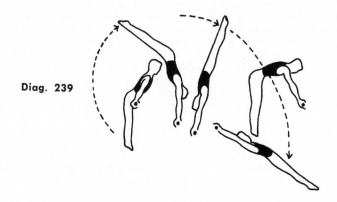

Diag. 239

c. Descend with a straight body and a flexed neck.

d. As body ascends, flex the hips and pull the bar toward the knees by extending the shoulder joint.

e. Release the bar at the *end* of the swing and dismount.

Spotting Suggestions

You should first teach the student to cast to a handstand from a low bar. Upon execution from the high bar, spot by slowing the boy down as he passes the median line. This can be accomplished by applying pressure on his buttocks. Also, when he dismounts, support his landing by grasping his waist with both hands.

7. *From a Hang, Cast to a Kip Up to Immediate Flank Vault Dismount to a Rear Even Stand* (4 points) (*Diag. 240*)

    a. Kip to a front support (refer to Junior Skills, Horizontal Bar No. 1).

    b. Cast backward off the bar as an extension of the kipping action.

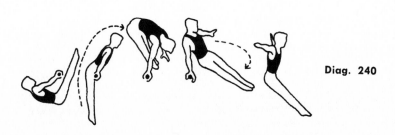

Diag. 240

    c. Raise the buttocks by flexing the hips and lean to the right side.

    d. Pass both legs over the bar, on the left side, and remove the left hand.

    e. Straighten the body as it passes over the bar by pushing with the right arm and extending at the hips.

Spotting Suggestions

The flank vault from the front support should be practiced on the low bar. Next, have the student execute a drop kip to a flank dismount. Upon attempting the skill on the high bar, stand in front of the student and be prepared to control him as he nears his landing.

Parallel Bars (suggested value 20 points)

1. *From a Cross Stand at Near End, Drop Kip to Lower Arm Support* (2 points) (*Diag. 241*)

    a. From a cross stand at the end, jump and swing body forward in a deep piked position.

    b. On the return swing, pull with both arms and "shoot" legs upward while extending the hips.

    c. Continue pulling and "shooting" until the shoulders are well above the bars. Swing to the rear in a lower arm support.

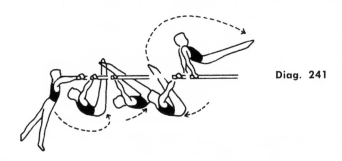

Diag. 241

Spotting Suggestions

You may guide the student to the lower arm support position by placing a hand on his lower back.

2. *From a Cross Upper Arm Support, Swing to a Front Up-rise* (2 points) (*Diag. 242*)
   a. Swing in upper arm support position.
   b. Flex the hips at the peak of the rear swing.
   c. Extend the hips on the downward swing.
   d. Push downward with upper arms, drive the hips forward and upward and swing to lower arm support. Swing to the rear in lower arm support.

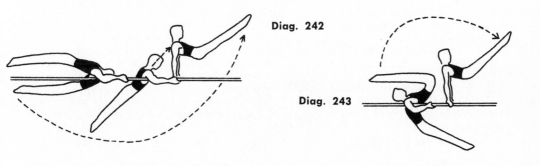

Diag. 242

Diag. 243

SPOTTING SUGGESTIONS

You may assist the student by pushing him into position as he rises in the front.

3. *From a Cross Upper Arm Support, Kip Up to a Lower Arm Support* (2 points) (*Diag. 243*)
   a. Swing to deep pike position in upper arm support.
   b. Snap legs forward and lift shoulders over point of support by pushing with the hands.
   c. Swing to the rear in lower arm support.

SPOTTING SUGGESTIONS

You may assist the student by supporting his lower back, reaching under the bars as he snaps forward.

4. *From a Cross Lower Arm Support, Swing and Execute Double Leg Cut Over One Bar on Rear of Swing* (2 points) (*Diag. 244*)

Diag. 244

a. Take a slight swing to the rear and hyper-extend the hips.
b. Push with the left arm, lean to the right, and swing both legs over the left bar.
c. Regrasp the left bar, with the left hand, and finish in a lower arm support.

SPOTTING SUGGESTIONS

Spot by grasping the performer's right upper arm and wrist, and support him through this movement.

5. *From a Cross Lower Arm Support, Swing Forward and Execute a Dip Half Turn to a Cross Upper Arm Support (3 points) (Diag. 245)*
    a. Swing to the rear in a lower arm support.
    b. Dip and swing forward.
    c. Push upward vigorously by extending the arms as the body rises in front. Release the left hand, look over your right shoulder and continue pushing with the right hand until the body starts the turning motion. Assist the body turn by releasing the right and moving the shoulder into a cross position with the bars. End in an upper arm support.

Diag. 245

SPOTTING SUGGESTIONS

Support the student by holding his legs and hips after the turn. You should always reach under the bars to aid the student. If the student is able to secure enough height on the forward swing, you can reach over the bars and support his legs after the turn is completed; however, you should exercise considerable *caution* when attempting to spot in this fashion. In addition, a mat can be placed over the bar upon which the student is turning into; in the illustration it would be the right bar. This mat is placed to correspond with the position of the legs after they complete the turn. In the event the student should turn too wide and come down on the right bar, the mat could support his landing.

6. *From a Cross Lower Arm Support, Swing to a Shoulder Balance and Execute One Back Shoulder Roll* (3 points) (*Diag. 246*)

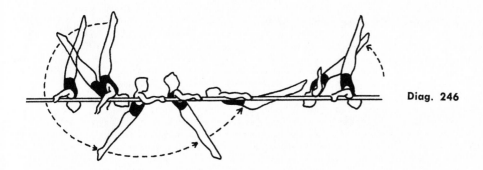

Diag. 246

a. Swing to shoulder balance from lower arm support.
b. Release the bars and swing downward.
c. Regrasp the bars, at the bottom of the swing, and push hips upward as the body swings forward.
d. Release bars and extend the neck while keeping arms stretched sideward.
e. Regrasp bars in the shoulder stand position.

You should support the student by pressing upward on his shoulders as he turns over backwards. This will prevent his slipping through the bars.

7. *Hold a Handstand on Low Bars or Parallettes* (*three seconds*) (3 points)
   a. Refer to Novice Skills, Floor Exercise No. 8.

8. *From a Cross Lower Arm Support, Swing and Execute a Double Rear Dismount to an Even Left Side Stand* (3 points) (*Diag. 247*)
   a. Take a slight swing to the rear in a lower arm support.
   b. Assume a slight pike at the peak of the backward swing.

Diag. 247

   c. Push with the left arm, lean to the right and swing both legs over the left and right bars. Both legs are snapped into a piked position from the pike at the rear of the swing.
   d. Regrasp the right bar with the left hand upon landing.

Refer to Advanced Skills, Parallel Bars No. 4.

Still Rings (suggested value 11 points)

1. *From a Piked Inverted Hang, Execute a Dislocate* (2 points) (*Diag. 248*)

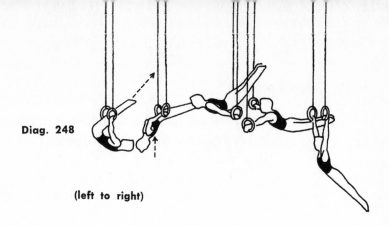

Diag. 248

(left to right)

a. Refer to Junior Skills, Still Rings No. 5.
b. The level of performance should be considerably improved. Note the back kip action which brings the body to a support position well above the rings.

Spotting Suggestions

This skill should first be practiced on the low rings. Figure 5 would set the student on the mat.

2. *From a Support, Lower to a Shoulder Balance* (4 points) (*Diag. 249*)
   a. Muscle-up to a support position.
   b. Raise legs to an "L" position.
   c. Slowly roll forward and raise the hips as high as possible.
   d. Place shoulders between the rings and arch the body.
   e. Maintain balance by manipulating the rings as the weight changes. Hold for three seconds and return to the starting position.

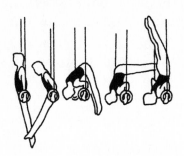

Diag. 249

Spotting Suggestions

This skill should first be practiced on the low rings to enable you to hold the performer's legs and adjust his position.

3. *From a Hang, Kip Up to a Support* (3 points) (*Diag. 250*)
   a. Assume a piked inverted hang position.
   b. Snap legs up, outward, and pull inward with both arms.
   c. Turn the rings outward as the shoulders pass above the elbow level. Push downward and straighten the arms.

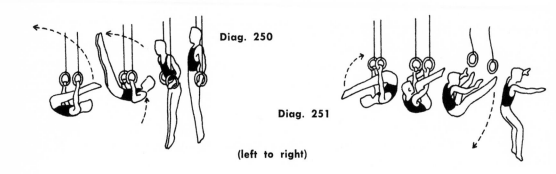

Diag. 250

Diag. 251

(left to right)

SPOTTING SUGGESTIONS

Practicing this skill on the low rings will allow you to push the student's lower back with one hand and support his lower legs with the other.

4. *From a Piked Inverted Hang, Swing to an Inlocate to an Immediate Front Double Leg Cut-off* (2 points) (*Diag. 251*)
   a. Swing to a piked inverted hand position.
   b. Cast forward and execute an inlocate; refer to Intermediate Skills, Still Rings No. 4.
   c. Immediately after inlocating, straddle legs over the wrists and go into a "rocking" type motion.
   d. Release both rings at the peak of the forward "rock" and straighten the body. Land with the legs together.

SPOTTING SUGGESTIONS

Refer to Intermediate Skills, Still Rings No. 4, for the spotting of the inlocate. Spot the double leg cut-off by supporting the student's waist from the rear as he rocks forward and releases the rings.

Tumbling (suggested value 10 points)

1. *Three Headsprings* (2 points)
   a. Refer to Junior Skills, Tumbling No. 1.
2. *Standing Back Somersault* (2 points) (*Diag. 252*)
   a. Jump as high as possible, in a vertical direction, with the hands completely elevated over the head.
   b. Just prior to reaching maximum height or reach, throw the head back (extension) and flex or tuck the legs tightly into the chest.
   c. To insure this tight tuck, hold the legs close with your hands.
   d. Three-quarters of the way around should be time enough to start opening the tuck and start to prepare for the landing. Upon landing, flex the knee to absorb the shock.

Diag. 252

(left to right)

SPOTTING SUGGESTIONS

Since this skill not only requires motor ability but also a definite kinesthetic sense, extreme care should be exercised when spotting this maneuver. You should first have the student practice jumping for height several times. Then have him jump and tuck. When attempting the exercise you should place your strongest arm in the ready position —the hand placed on the mid-portion of the spine. As the turn is completed, move your hand and replace it on his back. As the boy starts the jump, you should be prepared to help elevate his body by lifting the back. In the event the boy is unable to complete the turn, you must complete his rotary motion for him by "flipping" him around with your hand. During the early phases of learning the skill it is advisable to use the safety belt.

   3. *Three Back Handsprings or Flip-flops* (2 points)

      a. Refer to Junior Skills, Tumbling No. 3.

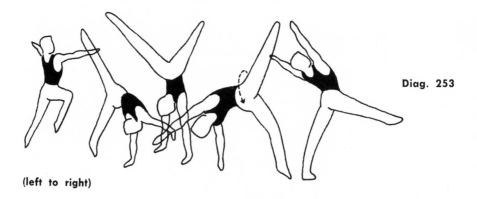

Diag. 253

(left to right)

   4. *Tinsica* (2 points) (*Diag. 253*)

      a. Step and hurdle.

      b. Kick through a cartwheel position.

      c. As the legs pass overhead, turn the hips outward a quarter turn.

      d. Step out by placing the left foot as close to the left hand as possible.

SPOTTING SUGGESTIONS

Assist the performer to stand up by placing your hand on his lower back after the quarter turn has been executed.

   5. *Round-Off, Back Handspring* (2 points)

a. Perform a round-off, as illustrated and described in Novice Skills, tumbling No. 5.

b. Pull both legs through, about 12 inches from the hands, so that the body weight is falling backward upon landing.

c. Immediately execute a backward handspring (Junior skills, Tumbling No. 3). Combine these parts without stopping.

Senior

Skills

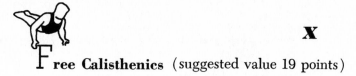

X

F**ree Calisthenics** (suggested value 19 points)

1. *From Handstand, Execute Half Pir-*
   ouette (2 points) (*Diag. 254*)
   a. Kick to handstand.
   b. Place body weight on the right
      hand.
   c. Push off the floor with the left
      hand and execute a quarter turn.
   d. Transfer body weight to the left

hand and immediately execute another quarter turn in the same direction.

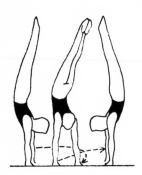

Diag. 254

Diag. 255

SPOTTING SUGGESTIONS

The student can be assisted by holding his legs as he attempts the pirouette.

2. *From Handstand, Lower to Immediate Headspring* (2 points)
    a.   Refer to Novice Skills, Floor Exercise No. 8.
    b.   Refer to Junior Skills, Tumbling No. 1, b, c, d.
3. *From a Scale, Kick Up to Handstand and Hold* (2 points) (*Diag. 255*)
    a.   Assume the scale position and hold for three seconds.
    b.   Lean forward, bend the supporting leg slightly and kick to a handstand. Hold.
4. *Press to Handstand with Bent Arms and Bent Legs* (3 points) (*Diag. 256*)
    a.   Assume a squat position with arms on the outside of knees.

Diag. 256

Hands are placed on the floor about shoulder width apart and fingers are spread.

b. Lean forward with bent arms and raise the feet off the floor.

c. Legs remain in a tight tuck position as the hips are raised above the head. The legs and hips are extended and the arms straightened after the hips are placed above the shoulders. Hold this handstand for three seconds.

SPOTTING SUGGESTIONS

The pupil can be assisted by supporting his legs as he attempts the stand.

5. *From Handstand, Execute Forward Roll with Straight Arms to a Stand with Straight Legs* (2 points) (*Diag. 257*)

   a. Kick to a handstand.

   b. Tilt the shoulders forward while keeping the arms straight.

   c. Keep hips as high as possible and flex the head prior to making contact with the floor.

   d. Roll up to feet by assuming a very deep piked position and pushing with hands, as illustrated.

Diag. 257
(left to right)

Diag. 258

SPOTTING SUGGESTIONS

Assist by holding the student's legs and walking him through the skill.

6. *Split* (3 points) (*Diag. 258*)

   a. Assume the position, as illustrated.

b. This is a skill that requires considerable stretching for long periods of time to acquire the flexibility that is so essential for its successful execution. Practice this movement by stretching as low as possible in this position at every workout.

SPOTTING SUGGESTIONS

You can have the student practice the "hurdle position" and gradually open up into the split. When attempting to lower down into the split position, have the pupil support the position with his hands, during the early phases of learning to avoid strains as well as sprains.

7. *Round-Off Back Handspring* (2 points)
   a. This is a combination of skills learned in a previous chapter.
   b. Refer to Advanced Skills, Tumbling No. 5.
8. *Tinsica, Round-Off Back Handspring* (3 points)
   a. This is a combination of skills learned in a previous chapter.
   b. Refer to Advanced Skills, Tumbling Nos. 4 and 5.

Long Horse (suggested value 6 points)

Horse in Cross Position (standard height)

1. *Stoop from Neck* (3 points) (*Diag. 259*)
   a. Run fast with a good forward lean.
   b. Dive forward with arms extended and eyes focused on the neck of the horse.

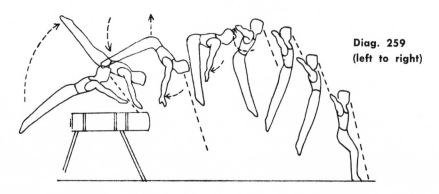

**Diag. 259
(left to right)**

c. The hands contact the neck, and the body is at a 30 degree environ. At the moment of contact, the arms should be pushing against the horse and the legs snapped downward by flexing the hips.

d. Increase the piked position until the legs are clear of the neck of the horse. The arms circle back-upward after the push.

e. Straighten the body as soon as possible for landing.

Spotting Suggestions

Spot by standing in front of the neck. As the student vaults, move in and support his landing by grasping him around the waist.

Side Horse (suggested value 12 points)

1. *From an Even Front Stand with Left Hand on the Neck and Right Hand on the Left Pommel: flank vault mount with half turn clockwise and continue swinging legs over the right pommel to a rear support over the saddle* (3 points) (*Diag. 260*)

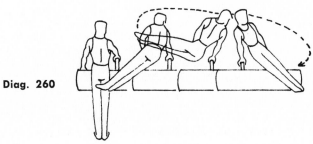

Diag. 260

a. Stand facing the horse, as illustrated, right hand with regular grip.

b. Jump upward, place body weight over right hand and push with the left hand.

c. Legs pass over the neck in piked position and over the crop and saddle in a semi-piked position.

d. Assume a rear support position.

Stand to the right side of the student and grasp his right wrist with your right hand and his upper arm with your left hand. As he starts the move, support his arm until the skill is accomplished.

2. *From Front Support Over the Saddle, Feint with Right Leg and Execute Two Double Leg Circles* (3 points) (*Diag. 261*)
   a. Assume a feint position, as illustrated.
   b. Swing the right leg backward.
   c. Join the legs in the rear and lean to the right as the legs pass over the left side.
   d. Pass through a stretched or extended rear support position, as illustrated (continue around once more).
   e. Lean to the left, pike slightly as the legs pass over the right side of the horse. Assume a front support position.

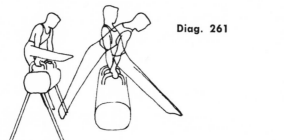

Diag. 261

Diag. 262

3. *From Front Stand at the Croup or Neck, Execute Two Double Leg Circles* (3 points) (*Diag. 262*)
   a. From an erect standing position, jump around the end of the horse to a rear support position and continue circling legs until a front support position is reached. Repeat. The body weight must be transferred from hand to hand as the legs pass over the horse.
   b. The position of the body (as seen in the illustration) should be complete extension at that particular point in the performance.

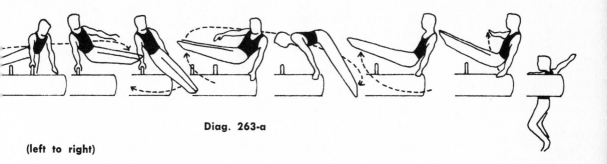

Diag. 263-a

(left to right)

4. *From Front Support Over the Neck: feint right leg and then swing both legs to a rear support and continue swinging over left pommel to a cross front support; continue to swing on neck of horse (cross position) over pommel to an even left side stand—loop off* (3 points) *(Diags. 263a, 263b)*

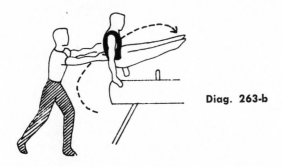

Diag. 263-b

a. Assume a feint position on neck of the horse.
b. Swing the right leg to the rear.
c. Join legs in the rear and continue swinging to rear support.
d. Execute a quarter turn and perform a circle while facing down the length of the horse.
e. Reset the left hand on the end, after the legs pass under it; push off to one side and dismount as the legs pass over the horse.

SPOTTING SUGGESTIONS

See illustration.

Horizontal Bar (suggested value 18 points)

1. *From a Light Swing with Regular Grip: cast and half-turn on the forward swing, change to a regular grip, and immediately kip-up to a front support* (3 points) (*Diag. 264*)
   a. Jump to the bar with a slight swing and cast with a half turn to the right side.

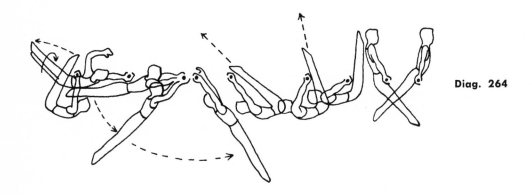

Diag. 264

   b. Regrasp the bar with the left hand in an over-grip and swing forward (right hand in reverse grip).
   c. At the end of the forward swing, change the right hand to an over-grip, bring the toes to the bar and kip-up to a front support.

SPOTTING SUGGESTIONS

Stand to the side of the pupil and as he executes the half turn on forward swing be ready to support his torso in the event his left hand does not regrasp the bar. Also, you should keep a careful watch when he is about to change the right hand from the reverse grip to the regular grip—this situation might call for your supporting his lower back and buttock area. It would be advisable to have the student practice the half turn on the chest-high bar first, before attempting to combine it with the kip-up on the high bar.

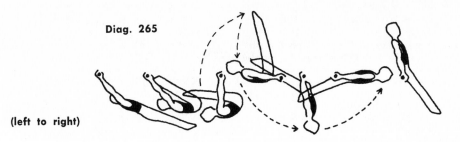

Diag. 265

(left to right)

2. *From a Light Swing Cast to a Back Kip to a Rear Support* (3 points) (*Diag. 265*)
   a. Cast and bring the legs between the hands on the forward swing (as soon as the hips reach their maximum "lift," pike the legs through immediately).
   b. Extend the legs upward as shown in the fourth figure.
   c. Drop backward in a deep piked position.
   d. Straighten the hip (extension) and finish in a rear support position.

SPOTTING SUGGESTIONS

This skill is similar to a backward seat circle from a rear support. It should be taught on the low bar and the spotter should be standing in front and to the side of the bar as the student starts the maneuver (this description will be from the student's right side). When he reaches position four, in the illustration, reach under the bar and support his thighs with your left hand, to prevent the legs from following the torso too closely, and support his chest with your right hand while lifting his chest and keeping his buttocks in contact with the bar. The purpose of the hand position is to "fix" his leg-hip angle with the left hand, and to move his back-hip angle to the 180° angle with the right hand (figure six). This type of execution will also serve as an important prerequisite for learning advanced skills that, at the straight body support position, require tremendous leg-hip flexion, such as the "German" giant swing.

3. *Two Regular Giant Swings* (4 points) (*Diag. 266*)
   a. Assume a front support position with a regular grip.
   b. Cast upward to a handstand position and under-balance.

c. Pike slightly as the body descends from the handstand.

d. Stretch out on the downward swing until the body reaches a vertical position.

e. "Pump" the hips upward as the body ascends on the forward swing.

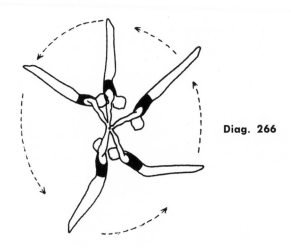

Diag. 266

f. Drive the body over the bar through the handstand by arching, and repeat the "action."

SPOTTING SUGGESTIONS

Once a student has mastered the three-quarters giant swing, the full giant is within his realm of learning. By the latter I am referring to physical development as well as mental attitude. The boy has to be told to maintain a straight body throughout the skill. The critical point will be at approximately three-quarters of the way around. At this point, unless he employs the proper body action (explanation e), he is going to descend rather than ascend to the handstand position. Therefore, you *must* stand directly beneath the bar and be ready to stop his downward fall (momentum) completely before his body passes the mid-point—or that position directly beneath the bar. If the boy is spotted after the mid-point he will most likely lose his grip and fall to the floor. If the student accomplishes the skill, instruct him to hold on and relax. It is advisable to stop his swing (after completing the first giant) at the mid-point, rather than have him go around a second time during the early stages of learning. This giant can also be spotted in the belt most effectively by using the overhead suspension. Make sure when the boy is in the "rig" and in front support position on the bar that the ropes go from the belt, around his waist, underneath the bar to the overhead attachment.

4. *Two Reverse Giant Swings* (4 points) (*Diag. 267*)
   a. Assume a front support position with reverse grip.
   b. Cast upward to a handstand and over-balance.
   c. Stretch the body on the downward swing and bend at the hips on the upward swing.
   d. Hold the piked position until the overbalance occurs, then stretch upward and repeat.

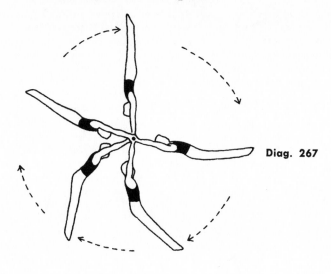

Diag. 267

SPOTTING SUGGESTIONS

This skill should be approached with caution because of the large swing that is necessary to circle the bar in a straight body position. The boy should have complete mastery of the three-quarters reverse giant before attempting this exercise. Once the boy attains the complete swing, it would be advisable to stop him at the mid-point (after descending from one complete swing) during the early stages of learning. It is best that he builds up his confidence and understanding before attempting multiple swings. For further suggestions, refer to Advanced Skills, Horizontal Bar No. 6, and Senior Skills, Horizontal Bar No. 3.

    5. *From Front Support, Cast to a Sole Circle Dismount to an Even Rear Stand* (2 points) (*Diag. 268*)

      a. Assume a front support position.

      b. Cast legs upward and straddle the bars, as illustrated.

Diag. 268-a: Front View

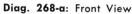
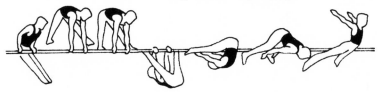

      c. Stretch backward and perform a three-quarter straddle turn.

      d. Flex the knees slightly and push off the bar with the feet.

      e. Raise the chest after releasing the bar and assume the stretch layout position before landing.

Diag. 268-b: Side View

SPOTTING SUGGESTIONS

This skill should be taught on a low bar with a very close spot. In spotting you should grasp the performer's wrist, on the last part of the turn, and guide him to the mat.

6. *From Rear Support with a Reverse Grip: lean to a forward seat circle to an immediate shoot-through to an even rear stand* (2 points) (*Diag. 269*)

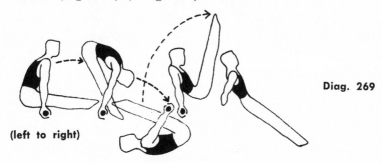

Diag. 269

(left to right)

   a. Assume a seat circle position with a reverse grip.
   b. Raise the hips upward and over-balance forward.
   c. Circle the bar once and maintain a deep piked position.
   d. Pull the hips over the bar and push off the bar for the dismount.

Spotting Suggestions

This skill should be taught on the low bar and the student should be guided throughout the move until he is in a standing position on the mat. You should first stand to the rear of the bar and hold the student's wrist with one hand and guide his upper back with the other (do not have him go over the bar at first, but rather have him end in the sitting position). Next, stand in front of the bar, and as he assumes the support position (after completing the circle), support his back and help lift him over the bar. Figure 4 should be carefully watched. At this point, the boy is likely to under-balance and would require assistance.

Parallel Bars (suggested value 32 points)

1. *From a Cross Stand at Near End, Straddle Mount to Lower Arm Support in "L" Position* (2 points) (*Diag. 270*)
   a. Grasp the end of the bars and jump upward.

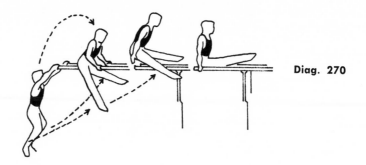

Diag. 270

b. Push downward with the arms and straddle legs on the outside of the bars. Both legs pass under hands.
c. Regrasp the bars and hold legs in an "L" position.

SPOTTING SUGGESTIONS

Assist by holding the student's waist from behind and supporting him until the "L" position is assumed. This skill should first be attempted on the low bars.

2. *From Even Front Stand with a Mixed Grip, Rear Vault to a Lower Arm Cross Rest Support in "L" position* (3 points) (*Diag. 271*)
   a. From an even front stand with a mixed grip:
   b. Jump and push vigorously with both hands while raising the hips and maintaining a piked position.
   c. Swivel the hips to the left (quarter turn) while releasing both hands to allow the body to pass into the cross position.
   d. Regrasp right hand to right bar and left hand to left bar and maintain the "L" position.

Diag. 271

During the early learning stages it is advisable to work on the low bars. Have the student practice the jump several times, then have him include the swivel motion (without removing his hand grip). When he is ready to execute the trick in its entirety, stand to his rear and place both hands around his waist. As he jumps, give him some support, then move in and place both arms beneath the bar to support his body as it passes into the cross position.

3. *From a Cross Stand Between Bars, Cast to Upper Arm Hang* (*no hold*) (3 points) (*Diag. 272*)
    a. Jump to support position and stretch body forward.
    b. Lean backward and swing downward.
    c. Assume a deep piked position and "drive" the seat upward over bars.

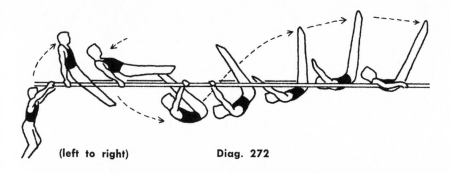

(left to right)   Diag. 272

d. Release bars from under position and place arms over the bars in an upper arm support.

Assist the performer by placing your hands on the performer's lower back and shoulders and guide him upward.

4. *From Cross Stand at Near End, Glide Kip to Lower Arm Support* (3 points) (*Diag. 273*)
    a. Grasp the ends of the bars and jump backward with hips leading.

  b. Swing forward with hips in a piked position. Straighten body at the end of the forward swing.

  c. Snap legs into deep piked position as the body returns rearward. Pull with arms and extend hips by shooting legs upward.

  d. Extend at the hips as the body rises over the bars. Swing in lower arm support position.

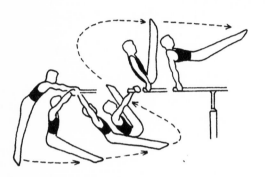

Diag. 273

(left to right)   Diag. 274

SPOTTING SUGGESTIONS

Assist the performer by pushing on his lower back as he rises above the bars.

  5. *From a Cross Stand at Far End, Back Kip to Lower Arm Support* (3 points) (*Diag. 274*)

  a. Stand, as illustrated, with hands in an outer grip.

  b. "Shoot" feet over head and pull the arms. Head remains flexed until the inverted position has been established.

  c. As the hips are thrown above the bars, the hands are changed to an over-grip above the bars. Straighten arms and swing forward in a lower arm support position.

SPOTTING SUGGESTIONS

This move should first be attempted on bars that are of medium height; this will enable the spotter to maintain full control of the situation.

Spot by standing to the student's right side: place your left hand around the boy's wrist (outer grip). As he "shoots" for the move, support the corresponding shoulder (figure 3).

6. *Swing to a Cross Handstand and Hold for Three Seconds* (3 points) (*Diag. 275*)
   a. Assume a light swing on the bars.
   b. Pike slightly in the forward swing and then swing the body up to the handstand, pivoting on the shoulders.
   c. As the body rises to the rear it should be slightly piked and when the balance is almost achieved the body is arched.
   d. Avoid an over-arched body, as shown in the illustration, and refer to Novice Skills, Floor Exercise No. 8, for further explanation.

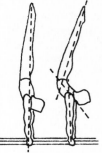

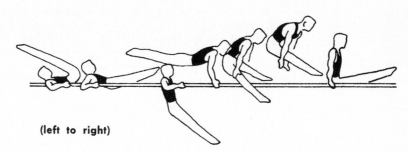

(left to right)

Diag. 275

Diag. 276

SPOTTING SUGGESTIONS

This skill should first be practiced on the low bars; bars are all the way down. As the pupil swings up, you can assist by supporting his legs and adjusting his shoulders, or by stabilizing his arm and his legs (posterior aspect) and by putting him into the correct position. You can also assist by stabilizing his arm and adjusting his shoulders, both on the ascent and the descent.

7. *From a Cross Upper Arm Hang, Swing to a Back Up-rise and an Immediate Double Leg Cut to an Upper Arm Hang* (3 points) (*Diag. 276*)
   a. Assume a piked inverted upper arm support position.
   b. Cast the legs forward to a straight body position.
   c. Pike as the body descends.

d. Hyper-extend the hips vigorously at the rear of the swing, push with the hands and straddle the legs over the bar.
e. The legs pass under the hands and over the bars.
f. Regrasp the bars with the legs in the "L" position and continue to swing.

SPOTTING SUGGESTIONS

As the boy straddles, you should be ready to move in, reaching in from under the bars, and by supporting his lower body as it starts to descend.

8. *From a Cross Upper Arm Hang, Cast to Back Up-rise and Immediate Half Turn Backwards to Upper Arm Hang* (3 points) (*Diag. 277*)
   a. Swing to inverted pike position.
   b. Cast forward and execute backward up-rise as described in Junior Skills, Parallel Bars No. 6.
   c. Hyper-extend the hips as the body reaches the horizontal position and execute a half turn by pushing with the hands. The right hand quickly reaches across and grasps the left bar for support as the other hand reaches across the chest for the other bar. Finish in an upper arm support position.

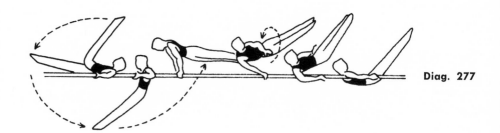

Diag. 277

SPOTTING SUGGESTIONS

Assist the student by supporting his back and hips after the turn.

9. *From a Cross Shoulder Balance, Execute Three-quarters Back Shoulder Roll to Immediate Front Up-rise* (3 points) (*Diag. 278*)

a. Assume a shoulder stand position.
b. Release bars with the hands and extend them to the side.
c. Pike slightly as the body descends. Grasp the bars and extend the hips as the body nears the vertical position.
d. "Drive" the hips upward, push downward with the hands, flex the neck and rise to a lower arm support.

Diag. 278   **Diag. 279**

SPOTTING SUGGESTIONS

You can assist the student by pushing his hips upward into position for the front up-rise.

10. *From a Cross Lower Arm Support, Swing to Double Rear Dismount with Half Turn in Pike Position, to an Even Right Side Stand (windee off)* (3 points) *(Diag. 279)*
    a. Swing to a three-quarters handstand position.
    b. Lean to the right and push off with the left hand.
    c. Assume a deep piked position and execute half turn.
    d. Change the grip on the supporting arm so the thumb is facing outward. Hyper-extend the hips before landing.

SPOTTING SUGGESTIONS

This trick can be spotted by standing to the side of the student and by grasping his right wrist and upper arm. Guide him throughout the execution of the entire move. This skill should be taught on the low bars.

11. *From a Cross Handstand, Quarter-turn to Squat Vault Dismount to Even Rear Stand* (3 points) (*Diag. 280*)
    a. Assume a cross handstand position.
    b. Shift the center of gravity to the left side by leaning to the left, and immediately transfer the right hand to the left bar while executing a quarter turn left.
    c. Keep shoulders over hands as the "heels" over-balance.
    d. Snap the legs downward into squat position and push with the hands, so the body is carried out away from bar.
    e. Stretch body before landing.

Diag. 280

SPOTTING SUGGESTIONS

This dismount should be taught on low bars. You should spot by grasping the performer's upper arm and pulling him outward.

Still Rings   (suggested value 14 points)

1. *From a Hang, Cast to a Back Kip to a Support* (3 points) (*Diags. 281a, 281b*)
    a. Jump to a hang with a regular grip.
    b. Shoot the body backward by pulling up with the arms and piking the hips.
    c. Extend the hips when the body has reached the piked inverted hang position (above the rings).

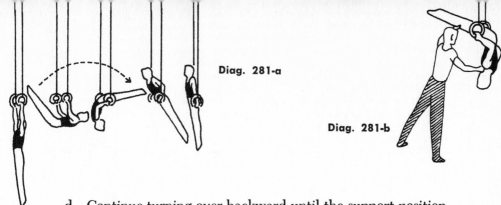

Diag. 281-a

Diag. 281-b

d. Continue turning over backward until the support position is assumed.

You may support the student's lower legs after the "shoot" has been performed. On shoulder height rings (where this skill should be first tried), when the student reaches the piked inverted hang and starts to "shoot," you may support his chest and legs, as shown in the illustration.

2. *From a Hang, Cast to a Back Up-rise to a Piked Support; Press to a Shoulder Balance* (3 points) (*Diag. 282*)

a. Assume a piked inverted hang position.

b. Cast legs upward and pull up with the arms.

c. Drive the legs and the hips downward to build up swing.

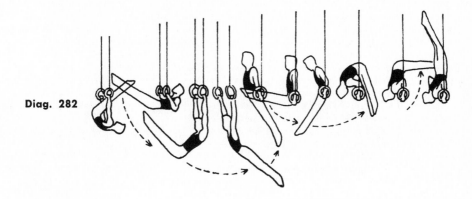

Diag. 282

d. Pull with the arms and come to a support position as the legs rise in the rear.

e. Raise the legs to the piked position and hold for three seconds.

f. Lean forward and press to a shoulder stand (refer to Advanced Skills, Still Rings No. 2).

187

SPOTTING SUGGESTIONS

You may assist the student to "back up-rise" by pushing his legs upward as he rises in the rear of the swing.

3. *From a Shoulder Balance, Lower to an Inverted Hang, Layout Position* (3 points) (*Diag. 283*)
   a. Muscle up to a support position.
   b. Press to shoulder balance (refer to Advanced Skills, Still Rings No. 2).
   c. Slowly lower the body between the rings to an inverted hang position. The head remains up or extended throughout the movement.

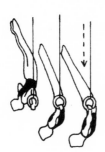

Diag. 283

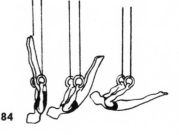

Diag. 284

SPOTTING SUGGESTIONS

Stand to the side of the student. As he lowers down to the vertical hang, guide his chest and back in the vertical plane.

4. *From an Inverted Hang, Lower to a Back Horizontal Hang and Hold for Three Seconds* (3 points) (*Diag. 284*)
   a. Assume a vertical hang.
   b. Slowly lower straight body to a horizontal position and hold for three seconds.

SPOTTING SUGGESTIONS

Give support to the boy's feet as he lowers into the horizontal hang. When dismounting, support his upper back. This move should be practiced on low rings when first learning.

5. *From a Hang, Swing and Execute a Backward Flyaway Dismount to an Even Rear Stand* (2 points) (*Diag. 285*)

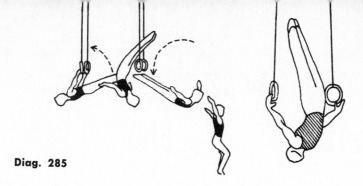

Diag. 285

a. Obtain a big swing from a hanging position.
b. Swing through the straight inverted hang position and release the rings.
c. Keep the body extended, arms straight and to the side, as illustrated (layout position).

SPOTTING SUGGESTIONS

Stand to the side of the student and be prepared to render support to his upper back should he over-rotate the skill; if under-rotation occurs, support his chest. This skill should first be practiced on medium height rings.

Tumbling (suggested value 9 points)

1. *Round-Off and Three Back Handsprings* (2 points) (*Diag. 286*)

   a. For round-off, refer to Novice Skills, Tumbling No. 5.

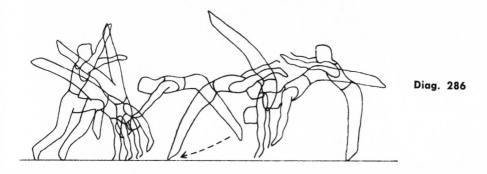

Diag. 286

   b. For back handspring, refer to Junior Skills, Tumbling No. 3; Advanced Skills, Tumbling No. 3.
   c. The round-off should flow into the back handspring.

Refer to Advanced Skills, Tumbling No. 3.

2. *Round-Off Back Handspring, Back Somersault* (4 points)
   (*Diag.* 287)
   a. Refer to Novice Skills, Tumbling No. 5, for the round-off
      and to Advanced Skills, Tumbling No. 3, for the hand-
      spring.

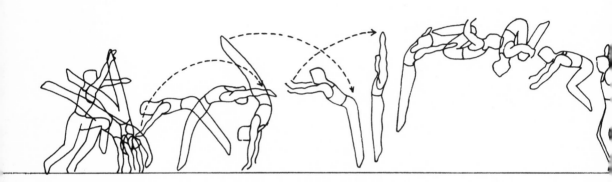

Diag. 287

b. The legs are snapped downward from the backward handspring and the chest is held high.
c. Rebound upward with straight legs and arms extended
   over head. Stretch upward with the entire body before
   throwing (neck extension) the head backward.
d. Pull the knees into the chest and look backward for the
   mat. Grasp the knees with the hands and hold them until
   you are ready to stand.

This combination of skills is best spotted in a belt. However, with
practice, you can learn to hand spot these movements by following
the student throughout the series and by holding his lower back during
the handsprings and the somersault (refer to Advanced Skills, Tumbling No. 2).

3. *Running Front Somersault* (3 points) (*Diag. 288*)
    a. Run forward taking small steps while staying high on the toes.

Diag. 288

    b. Jump very slightly forward and place feet together, immediately rebounding upward with a strong arm lift.
    c. Break downward with the arms, duck the head downward (head flexion) and grasp the knees tightly. Release the tuck and land upright.

Spotting Suggestions

This skill should be taught by first having the student somersault to a squat position on piled mats. The height of the mats will teach him to lift and turn over without fear of a hard landing. The front somersault may also be hand spotted by placing a hand on the performer's upper back after he ducks his head while attempting the forward maneuver.

Promoting

a Varsity

Gymnastics Team

XI

One of the most challenging assignments that I
have encountered in the field of physical education was that of promoting a gymnastics
team and giving it varsity status in the high
school's athletic program.

Gymnastics competition at my school,
like so many other schools, was virtually an
unknown sport. From past experiences I have
seen the values and benefits that a sound

gymnastics program can offer to a school's athletic program. On this basis I started out to promote and develop a varsity gymnastics team.

Prove a Need for a Program

One of the best means of promoting a newly organized gymnastics program is to show a need for it in your particular location with its own particular and peculiar situations. There are many basic principles that should be considered by the coach before he can justify his gymnastics program. However, the more important ones can only be determined by you, the instructor, after carefully scrutinizing your particular situation. (Refer to Chapter I, Scope of Progressive Gymnastics, for a more complete breakdown of basic considerations in setting up a program.)

In considering the principle "Meeting Individual Needs" (Chapter I), it should be noted that statistics reveal that approximately 30 percent of a school's student body participate in after-school athletics. This astounding fact might lead the taxpayer to think, "What are the other 70 percent doing?" After eliminating such factors as home chores and part-time jobs, there are still many boys who just stand on the side lines without rancor or jealousy and watch a handful of their peers always performing in sports. Still, you have a large majority of pupils who for some reason or other, do not fit into the school's athletic program which mainly emphasizes team sports or sports that require a specific prerequisite, as in swimming. Through aesthetically appealing gymnastics skills, an attempt is made to provide for the entire student, a development which comprises total fitness (physical, mental, emotional and social), and the enrichment of a maximum potential within each individual through the all-around gymnastics program.

After you have clearly considered and identified your basic principles, it is time to take the initial plunge into getting the gymnastics program sanctioned. If your department is governed by a chairman, he should be the first to hear of your idea. Invariably he will wish you "God's Speed," and advise you to consult the Director of Physical Education. At this point the novice coach might start to reminisce and wonder if his idea is really worth the effort. Do not be discouraged.

Good things never come easily. In most instances the Director will listen to your idea with sincere interest. Remember, improving the physical education and athletic programs not only increases your professional status but also adds professional distinction to the man in charge.

Financing the Program

Optimistically, let us assume that you have the "green light" to start a gymnastics program. The next major hurdle on the agenda is to find some way to finance the program. Many systems underwrite the entire athletic program for their participating schools, while others receive their equipment through a bonding process. If you as the coach can secure financing from one of the above methods, you are in "good shape." However, it is common knowledge that new athletic programs take time to be accepted, especially in the case of gymnastics.

At my school we followed a rather basic pattern. The principal was asked to allocate a certain amount of money from the high school's purchasing account to secure the necessary gymnastic equipment. (If your principal feels that his budget is too depleted to give you all that you desire, you might approach your Director; he is sometimes able to lend a helping hand through his contingency fund.) Once this request was granted, we then asked the Athletic Association, or General Organization, as it is sometimes called, to provide us with a budget for such items as uniforms, transportation, entry fees, and exhibitional supplies which included costumes, electrical supplies, etc. We received support from this organization mainly because the funds were made beneficial to the student body (in the form of a gymnastics team), and also because it enabled the group to organize in such a manner that they would eventually make up their financial deficit. The plan was to conduct a gymnastics exhibition by the high school's gymnasts.

This method of acquiring funds for newly formed groups also has application on the collegiate level. However, the initial soliciting is from the institution's Student Activities Association. The procedure is to organize a group of students, have them prepare a club constitution, and submit it to the Student Association (all formal clubs fall under the auspices of the Student Association). When the constitution is approved, the club may then formally submit its budget requesting financial assistance.

Securing Varsity Status

When the club can successfully maintain its membership and meet its competitive schedule, then it is time to make a request, to the Director of Athletics, for varsity status. If the request is granted, the club is usually placed on "trial" for one season by the Athletic Department. That is to say, the group must assume its own financial responsibilities (supplied from the Student Association) and meet a competitive schedule that is in conformity with the policy governing Intercollegiate Athletics at that particular institution.

Such a policy would probably list certain prerequisites for newly organized varsity teams. These might include meeting a minimum schedule with four-year institutions of higher education; this would make known to the department that the group has a sufficient number of matriculated students participating and that the club is able to secure competitive meets from recognized institutions. Another prerequisite might be to limit your schedule to a certain radius from the campus. This is to assure the Athletic Department that competition is readily available within your own vicinity or thereabouts, thus keeping future travel expense within the budgetary allocations as well as to conform with the school's philosophy governing intercollegiate athletics.

If the club adequately meets the "trial period" it then is admitted into the varsity ranks of the college. From this point on it will be under the sole jurisdiction of the Athletic Department. However, it would be very beneficial to maintain, as a separate organization, the group's club status. In this manner, the club member who does not choose to take part in the highly organized training and complex schedule of a varsity team can still fulfill his personal needs and desires (with respect to the activity) by maintaining his club membership with regulations less demanding than those of the varsity.

If the club's request for varsity membership is denied, because of one reason or another, it would be wise to continue as a club and re-apply for varsity membership in the near future.

Sources of Equipment

Another source of acquiring supplies and equipment would be to contact the senior class. Each year this group usually donates a gift to a department within the school. Many a high school's physical education program has been the beneficiary of some particular piece of equipment whether it be a score board for the basketball team or a trampoline for the apparatus program. Another reliable source might be the Parent-Teachers Association. If funds are available, this group is always ready and willing to lend a helping hand, provided you can justify your request. The best way to reach this organization is through the students themselves. A fund-raising campaign can be started in the classroom and climaxed in the meeting hall. At this rate the parents will have had time to think over your request. Once you feel certain that adequate finances are within the realm of possibility, your next step is to start forming an organized team.

Building a Team

Acquiring a team may not be as easy as some people think; the prospective coach will be competing against popular activities that have been part of the athletic program for many years, such as basketball, swimming and wrestling. However, with sufficient stimulation, an adequate turnout can be expected. One approach to the motivation of new students is to bring in a well trained high school or college team. This demonstration can be set up as an assembly program or an after-school special event. Posters could be made and a well-planned publicity program could be initiated to insure a large student body turnout. Many pupils will invariably be stimulated by the group and they will soon inquire as to the possibilities of their joining your group.

Another motivating device would be to show gymnastics films during assemblies or to put notices in the daily school's bulletin and hold the movie session after school. Still another method is to select outstanding performers from the physical educational program and invite them to one of your practice sessions. Almost any boy who seeks personalized attention (and what boy doesn't) will be a possible candidate for the gymnastics group. One major problem will be to find students who are truly sincere about the activity and not just out to satisfy a personal fancy. Remember, all that is needed is a nucleus. The rest will come in due time.

Introducing Progressive Gymnastics

Your next step as mentor is to introduce progressive gymnastics to develop skills at a rapid pace in the early stages of practice. The tyro gymnast, at this stage needs this stimulus to readily assure himself that he made no mistakes in going out for gymnastics. Boys are mainly looking for satisfaction and confidence. Above all, try to avoid unnecessary criticism especially if presented in an unconstructive manner. This sort of humiliation will only create a bad atmosphere. Following these few simple suggestions, the new coach will be able to draw from his novice crew a new and stimulating interest in gymnastics.

In the early stages of training, introduce the group to the many gymnastics events available. This should give you a good idea of their learning abilities which in turn would serve as a valuable tool, for both you and the boys, in selecting a single event where it would be most beneficial for them to start. By limiting the majority of a boy's workout time to one event, he will soon start to notice an increase in his general ability and thus an increase in his over-all interest. After he has made a definite accomplishment on a particular apparatus, move him to a second "piece." In this manner you will start to develop the all-around gymnast.

Competitive gymnastics can often prove to be very difficult, especially to a novice group. In order to give the team the necessary impetus required for its inception into the varsity category, it might be very wise to organize an exhibitional team in conjunction with the competitive group. In this manner you can still maintain public recognition while the team is ridding itself of "growing pains." Long horse vaulting, dance routines, double balance, marching drills, specialty acts and tableaux are typical examples of exhibitional gymnastics. Exhibitional training will prepare the team to perform before Parent-Teachers Associations, schools, student bodies, social institutions, and hospital recreational programs. A climax to your season's work could be a Home Exhibition for your own student body and their parents. A performance of this nature will surely convince the public that you have earned a rightful place in the school's athletic program.

Public Relations

Promotion of any newly organized group is greatly influenced by the public relations program that one undertakes. Generally speaking, the public is very interested in school affairs since children are the nucleus of all activities. One of the best places to start your informative campaign is in your own institution. The school's daily bulletins as well as their weekly or monthly paper could give your gymnastic team invaluable publicity. Some school systems publish a "chalk sheet" that goes out to all teachers. This, too, if properly handled, could spread your ideas to the entire system.

At this point it might be very wise to contact the town newspaper's sports editor. Local publicity makes for excellent public relations since most citizens read a daily paper.

In the early stages of promotion, make known your proposed plans as well as the goals that you have in mind. This will clearly define your gymnastics program to the public. Once the nucleus of a team has been formed, start scheduling competitive and exhibitional contacts. However, try to "book" contacts that are homogeneous with your group's ability. One person might have a strong enough team to compete the first year and on the other hand, it might be wise for another coach to have a purely exhibitional season until his gymnasts get their "feet wet." The prospective coach shouldn't have much trouble in getting a complete schedule. There are many schools, social institutions, recreational agencies and local adult groups that would welcome such a performance by your team.

Many of these contacts will be more than willing to sponsor the team. In fact there might be a few dollars left for your school's fund. However, it should be understood that the organization requesting the group should provide the team with transportation. In this manner the school's account will not be overdrawn. (This agreement will also put your principal at ease.)

It is also very important to publicize each and every engagement that your group is part of, whether it be a simple demonstration or a very involved competitive meet. Whatever the situation might be, ask the sponsoring group to send a little note to your principal or director in regard to the team's general performance and behavior. When some of these letters start coming in, your superiors will soon realize that you are contributing to the total development of the individual in a justifiable and educational manner; and that such a gymnastic program has substantial basis for a birth in the school's athletic program.

In considering the details presented, it is obvious that the degree of personal initiative on the coach's part will be a primary factor in the promotion of a varsity gymnastic team. Students and their parents will back your campaign. Don't hesitate to tread on this old but rather fertile ground.

A History

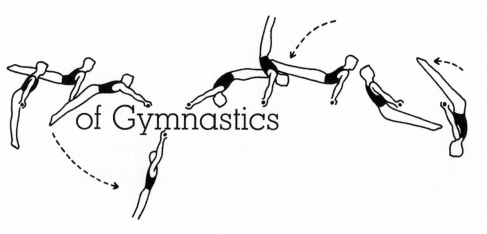

of Gymnastics

to the 19th Century

he development of gymnastics has been closely related with the forward progression in the history of education. It has been thought by many philosophers that when the physical vigor of a people has fallen low its educational level has also gone down. During such periods the scholars have turned their thoughts in the direction of improvement of the nation's strength-building factors; they see in them an unprecedented means of enhancing the whole individual.

The precursors of the gymnastics movement and physical education as a whole were found to be the philosophers and social leaders rather than the typical school men. Physical activities were grudgingly given birth in the educational curriculum and there are still a multitude of objections being exerted against the program. Its inception into the school's program has been due mainly to social pressure from outside groups. Throughout the years, in war as well as in peace, man has become educated to the idea that *physical education* is an important aspect of the total educational program, and gymnastics—a vital donor to growth and development—makes a significant pedagogical contribution to the development of the whole child.

The historical account contained within this chapter signifies a chronological approach to the propagation and to the interpretation of gymnastics. Its evolution has been influenced by countries, states, cities, institutions, groups and individuals in accordance with the "trends of time" throughout the history of mankind.

Egypt 2000 B.C.

Gymnastics became part of man's civilized culture as early as 2000 B.C. Interpretations of various paintings, vases, mosaics, and writings indicated that the Egyptians engaged in gymnastic games; for the more skilled, tumbling and other gymnastic stunts became the mode of participation.

Greece

The Homeric Greeks 1000 B.C.–800 B.C.

The Homeric Greeks strove for one major aim in education: individual excellence. This was accomplished by developing "Men of Action" and "Men of Wisdom." Its empirical meaning was carried into their physical education program where the major purpose was to develop the soldier. Prevailing situations compelled the early Greeks to center their exercises around the development of skills and qualities needed for military survival. However, their creative imaginations and competitive spirit gave rise to a multitude of dual and individual activities that has had direct influence on many of the twentieth century physical activities. They also gave new meaning to activity—the spirit of sportsmanship, the love of sport and the satisfaction of accomplishment became desired goals.

Gymnastics during early times was rather informal and the majority of events were associated with religious festivities. *The Illiad* and *the Odyssey* give indication that only men of noble birth participated in such sporting activities.

Sparta 800 B.C.–700 B.C.

The State assumed absolute responsibility for the education of its children; therefore, each adult citizen was considered a teacher. These residents or tutors selected certain young proteges, according to their worthiness, and trained them in gymnastics, an activity considered integral in the Spartan training program. Its primary purpose was to develop the "Man of Action," a quality essential to Sparta's rise to military supremacy.

As the child's physical education progressed, the gymnastic movements became more intensified in both severity and difficulty until he entered the final stage of the training program called the *Agoge*. This system was characterized by an ascetic and stoic type of training where young men, supervised by the *paidonomous*, or superintendent, had to endure hardships and discomforts to prove their worth and obedience to the State.

During this training stage, Greek law prescribed that the youths engage in the dance. One such dance was the "pyrrhic," a military dance, performed by naked children armed with the implements of war; the dance and gymnastic patterns resembled the maneuvers of the battlefield. These same naked youths had to pass-in-review for *Ephors*, or state officials, whose duties were to determine if the marchers' physiques were up to standard as a result of their gymnastic training.

On various festive occasions, Spartan youths were invited to exhibit their gymnastic skills. Often these festivities were in honor of Apollo—god of light and trust and patron of gymnastic games. Their gymnastic ability was also demonstrated in the Olympic Games where for many years they monopolized the competition. The State's success in Olympic competition, along with their disciplinary training methods such as the "pyrrhic" and reviewing before the *Ephors* gave the interpretation "naked art" to the word gymnastics—a symbol that has influenced many later civilizations.

Early Athenian Greeks 700 B.C.–400 B.C.

Early Athenian physical education was quite erratic of the Spartan system. The home became the medium for care and education of the infant, the general attitude being to develop both mind and body for war and for peace. Unlike Sparta, Athens combined the philosophy of "Men of Action" with "Men of Wisdom."

The Greeks in educating their young placed emphasis on music and gymnastics. Music was mainly utilized as a means for educating the mind; the main subject in the schools was the recitation of poetry with an accompaniment. Gymnastics, which was taught at the *Palestra*, a school for physical education, gave insight and meaning for that means which was gained through physical exercise. This particular culture thoroughly understood the ideology of "clear mind and healthy body" and its implication to the interdependence of physical and mental growth of the individual. Emphasis was placed on body perfection through aesthetically appealing skills. Beauty of execution and ease of performance took precedence over setting records and exhibiting feats of strength.

The *Palestra* also gave rise to an individualistic type of gymnastics, as opposed to a team effort, by homogeneously grouping its pupils and allowing them to participate in a progressive type of training. Their perception of the aims of gymnastics was: *Euxi* and *Eutaxi*. By the *Euxi* they understood good conditioning of the body and its entire well-being; by the *Eutaxi* they understood the discipline of the human being and good conduct mainly pertaining to the discipline of man in his sociological environment. It was during this era that Grecian physical education reached its zenith.

Late Athenian Greeks 400 B.C.–300 B.C.

The successful culmination of the Persian Wars helped to bring about the Golden Age of Athens. This hedonistic era placed major emphasis on *man*. "Satisfy the man" became the popular slogan. This attitude carried with it a scholastic concept that deemphasized physical education. "Men of Wisdom" soon became the mode of education.

This physical deterioration of the Greek populace saw the degeneration of gymnastics. The *Palestra* turned into a headquarters for professional athletes and their trainers. Medical gymnastics was administered mainly for care and prevention of injuries for those professionals engaged in the competition. The general public's participation consisted of mild exercises, viewing the professional train, and attending the baths.

The tendency toward professionalism destroyed the sporting atmosphere throughout Greece. The victor's crown of the sacred wild olive gave way to a more material reward and soon the athlete trained beyond natural limits to share in the monetary remuneration. The importance of the amateur athlete was soon diminished; for the ordinary competitor found it very difficult to engage with the professional. The plebiscite rose in opposition to this trend, but to no avail. When Philip of Macedonia defeated the Athenians at Chaeronea, the Greeks reevaluated the need for such physical training and erected the *Ephebic College* (335 B.C.) It was a two-year compulsory training school for young men between the ages of 18 and 21 whose program consisted of military tactical training and gymnastics. The specialized method of "Men of Wisdom" still remained very popular and was a major contributor to the one-sided development of the human body; a concept which disregarded the old Greek ideal of the perfectly proportioned physique.

Rome

Early Romans 300 B.C.–146 B.C.

The Republic of Rome was very militaristic in nature. The main objectives in teaching were limited to health, courage, strength, endurance, and skills for war. Being a very practical type of people they participated in gymnastics for specific military purposes, and disregarded the Grecian concept of the "Whole Man."

Unlike the Spartan and Athenian children, the Roman youngsters received their training in the home under the guidance and direction of their parents. The father often took his child to the *Campus Martius*, an outdoor school for physical training, and taught him the skills of battle through the medium of gymnastics as well as other skillful movements. Parental efforts in educating their young bore much fruit, for the Latins had sown the seeds of victory that were soon to develop into a tremendous empire, one unsurpassed in modern civilization, when they defeated the Hellenes.

Later Romans 146 B.C.–395 A.D.

The inception of the Roman Empire witnessed the adoption of a Grecian type culture. However, the trend was strictly scholastic in nature and very little emphasis was placed on gymnastic activity. Formulation of a professional army had further decreased the importance of civilian physical training; furthermore, the absence of a need of protective strength for service to the State gave play the impetus to become an end in itself.

The erection of the *Colosseum* aroused a spectator interest in Rome; plagued by repeated wars, the Empire chose to watch the sanguinary battles in the amphitheatre rather than engage in the exercises of the *palestra*. The plebes had come to regard sports as a popular means of entertainment with little regard to its contribution to educational endeavors. Although the Latins abducted the cultures of the peoples they vanquished, and transmitted them to the world, they seemed to have had little regard for gymnastics; it can be assumed that this physical activity did not provide this particular culture with the spontaneous reward, the quick and measurable results of accomplishment and the satisfaction that their utilitarian minds often demanded.

The Chinese 200 B.C.

The Chinese employed a series of mild corrective exercises called *cong fu* which shows a correlation to Ling's Swedish system. The Orientals believed that human life could be extended by maintaining and enhancing one's organic functions through a series of medical gymnastics which included stretching and breathing exercises.

Middle Ages and Early Modern Times
476 A.D.-1500 A.D.

The Dark Ages witnessed the fall of formalized gymnastics. The only indication of gymnastics during this era appeared within the social disciplines (1000 A.D.-1500 A.D.). This phase of the Middle Ages was characterized by a dignified system of education known as chivalry. It was in essence a moral and social code that evolved among the privileged nobles of the armed cavalry. The ultimate achievement of chivalric education was the conferrence of knighthood.

Preparatory training for knighthood required that pages and squires participate in vigorous gymnastics. These skills included basic movements and also the execution of various tumbling maneuvers while attired in full armor. The skills were believed to provide the necessary physical conditioning that was required for combat.

Gymnastics was also employed by entertainers when they demonstrated at elaborate court functions and when they were invited to the various castles to entertain the nobles. The gymnasts were said to have thrown wonderful somersaults and perform daring feats by leaping through hoops placed at certain distances from one another.

The Renaissance 1500 A.D.-1700 A.D.

Humanism

The Renaissance brought forth a humanistic movement that emphasized the development of the "whole man." They sought to establish a "sound mind in a sound body."

The inception of this movement took place in Italy: the ancient Roman ruins, the Latin language and the exodus of Greek scholars to that peninsula made it a natural "homing ground" for the revival of mental and physical activities.

An avid proponent of the gymnastic movement was the humanist Vittorino da Filtre (1370-1461). His school, *La Giocasa* (translated, it literally means "The Pleasure House"), was established primarily for children of wealthy parents; included within his curriculum was an organized gymnastics system whose purpose it was to enhance the physical fitness of local residents who were not of military age.

Moralism

The Reformation movement exemplified one of the most intricate conversions of modern times.

Religion became the basis of all study within the institutions of the Reformation. The reformers Martin Luther and Ulrich Zwingli both advocated the inculcation of limited gymnastics training into the educational curriculum; their programs were constructed similar to that of the antiquated Greek *palestra.*

Eighteenth Century Revival of Gymnastics
1776-1811

The eighteenth century, known as the Age of Enlightenment, marked the rebirth of physical training into the educational curriculum.

Jean Jacques Rousseau (1713–1778)

A philosopher, Rousseau, paved the way for the reappearance of this phase of education. The publication of his educational treatise in 1752, entitled *Emile,* depicted the value of a child's freedom from a sociological bondage and favored the natural development of his personality. The text also cried out, "the weaker the body the more it commands; the stronger it is the better it obeys—a debilitated body enfeebles the soul." Rousseau's educational procedures were so contrary to those being employed at that time that they attracted the interest of many school masters as well as members of the medical profession. Zukert, a doctor in Berlin, supported the premise that such activities as wrestling, vaulting, and swimming made a significant contribution in terms of hygenic values to children.

Rousseau's educational naturalism not only motivated eighteenth century education but also exercised a prodigious influence over contemporary civilization. His indefatigable and passionate rhetoric emphasizing the importance for body training earned him credit as being the instigator of its revival.

Johann Bernhard Basedow (1723–1790)

A German, Basedow was the first school master to administer a curriculum based on Rousseau's theory. It was at Soröe, Denmark, where his teachings attempted to relate the education of the mind and the body. He became so overwhelmed with his training program which coordinated the physical with the mental that he returned to Germany and founded the *Philanthropinum*, a school for the purpose of further crystallizing the idea of a naturalistic education. A prospectus issued in 1774 stated that the school day consisted of five hours devoted to studies, three hours devoted to exercise, and two hours devoted to manual labor. The traditional knightly exercises of fencing, dancing, and vaulting were first employed by Basedow; however, Johann Friedrich Simon, the physical education instructor, gradually enhanced the program by introducing in 1776 a series of "Greek Gymnastics" comprised of running, jumping, and throwing.

During the latter part of the eighteenth century, several new institutions were designed after Basedow's *Philanthropinum*. The most famous of these schools was the Schenpfenthal Educational Institute founded by C. G. Salzmann (1744–1811). Christian Carl André organized the instiution's first physical education program. He taught such activities as: pole vaulting, running, and various games. He is credited with introducing many of the exercises that comprise the present free exercise event in gymnastics.

Guts Muths (1759–1839)

Muths succeeded André as physical education instructor in 1786. His purposes were very similar to those of Rousseau. Mind and body were highly emphasized with total health rather than bookish learning being the primary objective. His main objective in teaching gymnastics was to create harmonious unity of mind and body. Muths divided his program into three classes: gymnastic exercises, manual labor and games of a social nature. In his text, *Gymnastics for Youth* (1793), which was the *first* written work of modern gymnastics, he describes his program as containing the sloping beam, climbing pole, rope ladders and climbing ropes, various balance exercises and exercises on the swinging beam. In short, his exercises were adapted to the characteristics of the individual and to the natural environment—a freedom of expression. Muths' efforts to develop a classified progression of gymnastic exercises for youth won for him wide acclaim as well as the unique distinction of being named "Grandfather of Gymnastics."

Because of the trials and tribulations of men like Rousseau, Basedow and Muths, the Era of Enlightenment gave gymnastic activity more attention than it had witnessed at any other time since the days of the ancient Greeks.

Pestalozzi (1746–1827)

Contrary to Rousseau, Pestalozzi believed that exercise programs should be promoted from a racial type of activity to a social type of activity. Like Basedow and Muths, he set out to introduce a progression program of gymnastics in the schools' physical education curriculum. His pedagogical gymnastic system was formulated to meet the abilities and limitations of individual body types as well as to combine the physical, mental and moral aspects of education. "The essence of elementary gymnastics," wrote Pestalozzi, "consisted in nothing else than a series of exercises of the joints, in which is learned, step by step, all that the child can learn with respect to the structure and movements of the body and its articulations." This explanation suggests that Pestalozzi's exercises closely resemble the present free calisthenic movements; also, it gives indication that Pestalozzi was introducing a mechanical method, subject to artificial control, as opposed to a natural and functional type of movement.

His concept of physical education has had tremendous implication on modern day programming. Present kinesiological studies of various motor movements stem from his early beliefs; also, his concepts have shed considerable light on the area of remedial physical education. His recognition of the importance of individual differences was in one respect a cultivation of the present educational ideology that children should not be spurred to strive to attain their peers' achievements but rather to measure progress in terms of individual growth. Finally, his cognizance of the moral as well as the physical and mental aspects of education leads one to assume that the philosophy of the world's finest Physical Education Teacher Training School, namely Springfield College, was directly influenced by Pestalozzi's teachings when they adopted the triangular philosophy of spirit, mind and body—education through the physical rather than of the physical.

Gymnastics

in Modern Europe

XIII

D enmark

Franz Nachtegall (1777–1847)

Nachtegall, the precursor of the gymnastics movement in Denmark, erected in 1799 the first modern institution in physical education which was organized specifically for instruction in physical skills. Nachtegall was a dedicated advocate of the public schools serving as the medium for instruction in gymnastic activity. He believed this to be essential if the growing generation was to benefit from the activity's contribution to the individual's total growth.

In 1804, Frederick VI, recognizing the actitvity's military significance, erected the Military Gymnastic Institute and appointed Nachtegall as its first superintendent. The school became so successful that the state erected the Civil Gymnastic Institute; this later was augmented and converted into the State Gymnastic Institute which became the first school where students could major in physical education. The Institute's scholastic influence led to the passing of a school bill in 1814, which made gymnastics compulsory for boys in the Danish schools; Nachtegall's text, *A Manual of Gymnastics for Elementary Schools*, was also sanctioned by the King to be the text for the course of study.

The inception of the Military Gymnastic Institute, which still exists, and is the oldest gymnastics institute still in operation, had direct influence on the German and Swedish schools of gymnastics.

Sweden

Per Hendrick Ling (1776–1839)

Traveler, poet and dramatist, Ling pioneered the development of Swedish gymnastics which has resulted in the most concise system of exercise ever known.

Motivated by the Napoleonic wars and the invasion of Russia, Ling, a patriot, devised a system of gymnastics designed for military purposes. Utilizing Nachtegall's system (which he had studied previously) and Muths' text, *Gymnastics for Youth*, he started to fulfill his altruistic desires. In 1805, as instructor at Lund University, he taught the Nachtegall system of gymnastics stressing precision of timing and correct execution. He soon became very interested in the physiological aspect of exercise and very shortly thereafter started to devote his entire attention to the "medical gymnastic" program.

Ling was instrumental in organizing the Royal Central Institute of Gymnastics in Stockholm in 1814, as well as developing three interrelated systems of gymnastics which sought to develop unity as their common basis: his physiological or pedagogical gymnastics strove to unite the various parts of the organism; his military gymnastics strove for unity between the body and the weapon in relation to the action of the opponent; and his medical gymnastics strove to restore unity between parts of the body which had been lost through "abnormal" conditions. Ling also gave some consideration to an aesthetic gymnastics; however, this was left to be developed in more modern times.

Of prime significance was his initiative in introducing the scientific approach to physical education. Ling contended, "if one is to develop the human body through gymnastics, then one must know that body." His study of body movement, as related to the anatomical and physiological, established it as a science, and through its alliance with the laws of physics, the seeds of future research were planted.

Hjalmar Frederick Ling (1820–1886)

Son of Per Hendrick Ling, he was dedicated to continue in his father's footsteps as a leader in the development of the Swedish gymnastic movement. His teachings emphasized mass body activity, as in the free exercise event, as well as mass body development.

Hjalmar's prime contribution to gymnastics was the *Gymnastic Day's Order*. These were progressive and classified gymnastics lesson plans that were graded for pupils of all ages and abilities. This system, along with some 2,400 pen and ink drawings of gymnastic positions and exercises, were adopted by the schools of Sweden; his contribution was also valuable in helping to formulate the mode of gymnastics both past and present in the United States.

Germany

Friedrich Ludwig Jahn (1778–1852)

Germany, at the birth of the nineteenth century, was comprised of some 300 cities and states. When the Prussians were forced to yield to Napoleon's army after the battle of Jena, and signed the Treaty of Tilsit, the sovereignties of the Deutschland suffered a tremendous setback thus depleting the country's morale and unity.

Jahn, a Prussian by birth and a teacher by profession, was one of education's most outstanding patriots. His energetic endeavors to create strong nationalistic feelings among the German people following Prussia's defeat by France, were unsurpassed. He employed physical education, namely gymnastics, as the medium for fulfilling his goals. His motto, *"frisch, frei, frohlich, fromm,"* which connotes, "free in spirit, strong in body, cheerful, intelligent and dependable" was lauded by his countrymen. His peers recognized him as "the apostle of German unity, the champion of liberalism, and the defender of the common man." And rightly so, for Jahn, a nationalist, believed in teaching fundamental skills and racial activities. His system of exercise as described in his text of 1816, *Die Deutsche Turnkunst* (meaning German Gymnastics), included: walking, running, jumping, vaulting over apparatus, exercises on the horse and buck, climbing, throwing with arm or sling, tug of war, games, and individual and dual stunts. He had no tolerance for the free exercise movements known at that time as *"Gelenkubungen"* (exercises of joints and muscles), utilized by Basedow and Pestalozzi. "Why extend the arms toward objects that are not there?" said Jahn. "Every exercise should have counter forces like climbing, throwing stones, etc."

Jahn perferred to call gymnastics *"Turen,"* a native word meaning gymnastics and exercises, whose root has become the basis for many other German terms. In 1811 he instituted the *Turnplatz,* a playground for public physical education. Soon after, he instituted the *Turnverein,* a gymnastics organization established to promote national strength and unity and to recreate the feeling of self-respect among the German people. Through physical education he hoped to reinstate the moral and physical aspects of life. Unlike Guts Muths, Jahn set out to achieve his goals by planning his gymnastics program for the adolescents *and adults* of the "fatherland," rather than centralizing the program around children and educational institutions.

Gymnastics became so popular that Jahn was confronted with a need for outdoor apparatus. He and his students solved the problem by building crude pieces of equipment which included: horizontal bar, parallel bar, vaulting horse, balance beam, inclined ladder, springboard, and other special apparatus upon which students could perform various exercises. His equipment, designed primarily for adolescents and adults, was installed in the various *Turnvereins* and his system of German gymnastics was exclusively employed.

The nobility honored Jahn for his efforts to unite Germany and free it from French control; however, once this was accomplished the citizens became very cautious of his overly liberal philosophy. Metternich failed to share Jahn's altruistic views and set out to subdue his physical education activities. In 1819, Jahn was arrested on charges of treason and was imprisoned for two years at Spandau. Following his release he remained under surveillance and was prohibited from teaching. During this time the Prussian government as well as several other German states became opposed to the *Turnverein*. Before long, the organization that Jahn had founded became all but extinct.

Jahn did not live to see the revival of gymnastics. Its rebirth, due to an increase of participants, lack of trained personnel, and the intellectual and military pattern of Prussia, made a transition from the fundamental and national to the artificial and highly formal.

History, recognizing Jahn as one of its dedicated disciples, has bestowed upon him the title of "Father of Gymnastics."

Adolf Spiess (1810–1858)

A native of Hesse, Germany, he was trained in both the Guts Muths and Jahn systems of gymnastics. Being a member of the *Turnverein* for many years, Spiess recognized the importance of gymnastics in the German school system. He visualized the activity as a pedagogical and concrete aspect of school life. It was his belief that apparatus exercises in the schools should be the means of educating the body, in the same measure as the other branches educated the mind.

For 15 years, while teaching in Switzerland, Spiess experimented with new ideas and new methods of gymnastics that would be appropriate for children. His experiment proved successful and the result was a progressive series of exercises and games of all kinds that were an expression of his aims of producing coordinated body development and habits of obedience. In 1848, upon his return to Hesse, his system was welcomed by a large number of school masters. His course of study was planned for boys and girls between the ages of 6 to 16 years of age and the skills included: marching, free exercises, swinging exercises, rope exercises, jumping exercises, dumbbell exercises, buck vaulting, hanging and supportive exercises and dancing. His success in introducing gymnastics into the schools of Germany was largely due to the fact that his objectives were synonymous with the despotic governmental and educational philosophy of the time.

Unlike Jahn, Speiss placed emphasis on formal activities; play activities were given a minor role. He proclaimed, "Here as everywhere else, the pupil must first learn what it is to obey, before he is allowed to do as he pleases." The utilization of gymnastics taught children how to practice and display discipline; of importance was the fact that he believed this to be true for both girls and boys.

Spiess' system of school gymnastics rapidly spread to neighboring countries. This movement served as the fuse for a long and bitter controversy over the two systems of gymnastics: Jahn versus Spiess. Ling's inception of the Swedish system of gymnastics served as the impetus to proclaim Spiess' progressions the more popular. All of the schools and the majority of the clubs prior to 1860 had formalized his program of gymnastics.

Spiess, known as the founder of German gymnastics, had laid the foundation for the formal exercises as they are known today, The kip-up, the giant swing, the flyaway, the emphasizing of the cliches ("toes straight, watch your form") all have had their derivation in the Spiess school.

Czechoslovakia

The purpose of gymnastics in Czechoslovakia, as in Germany, lay deeply rooted in nationalism. In an effort to free themselves from a despotic empire, the Czech gymnasts, under the leadership of Dr. Miroslav Tyrs and Jindrich Fugner, established, in 1862, the *Sokol* (Falcon) organization. Its pledge required that all members be faithful to the ideals of "freedom, equality, brotherliness, and a love of country."

This patriotic gymnastics movement has evolved more than 750,000 members who belong to 3,150 clubs, which have at their disposal 1,100 well equipped gymnasiums. Today, these voluntary

Sokol branches flourish in nearly all Bohemian countries throughout the world. Similar to the *Turners*, the *Sokols* are primarily concerned with moral, aesthetic and intellectual development as well as the physical components of the "whole man."

Denmark

Niels Bukh (1880–1950)

Proclaimed as a modern contemporary teacher of gymnastics, Bukh established himself at the Folk High School of Physical Training at Ollerup.

He developed a "primitive" or "fundamental" type of gymnastics which utilized vigorous, rhythmical, free flowing and continuous movements that emphasized intensive stretching to seek elasticity and flexibility. Span-bending, heaving, balancing and breathing exercises, characteristic of the Swedish system, were omitted to make way for three main types of physical development: flexibility, strength, and coordination.

In lieu of such heavy apparatus as the beams, benches, Danish horse, and the buck, Bukh employed the wall bars, vaulting boxes, and Danish agility mattresses. His classes were approximately 45 minutes long and comprised marching, free exercise for 30 minutes, concluded with agility work vaulting and marching to a cadence around the gymnasium while chanting a spirited song.

The essence of his program was concerned mainly with correcting undesirable body positions and uncomfortable muscular effects derived from certain types of farm labor.

The Danish gymnastics system appeared in the United States in 1923 when Bukh and several of his students were on tour of the States. His program was adopted mainly by high school and college women, from 1925 to 1930; however, the males found considerable value in Danish gymnastics when utilized for preseason conditioning exercises for athletic squads. During World War II, Bukh's system was an essential part of the Armed Forces training program.

Gymnastics

in the United States

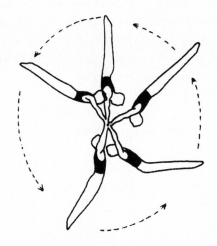

XIV

National Period*

Gymnastics was introduced in America 14 years after the inception of the *Turnplatz* at Hasenheide, by three proteges of Friedrich Jahn who sought political asylum in the United States. Charles Frollen (1796-1840) and Charles Beck (1798-1866), both refugees from Germany, were the first to arrive.

The Round Hill School in Northampton,

---

* The period from the American Revolution to the Civil War.

Massachusetts, hired Beck as an instructor of Latin and of gymnastics. Being an avid gymnast, he organized, in 1825, an outdoor gymnasium whose primary purpose was "to furnish opportunity and means of exercise to the youth of the city." His program was modeled after the Hasenheide *Turnplatz* and his dedicated efforts in gymnastics were eventually proclaimed as significantly contributing to development of the school gymnasium movement in America.

Frollen was hired by Harvard College as a pioneer instructor in German. His deep seated interest in the teachings of Jahn soon found its way into his leisure time activity and it soon spread to a vast majority of the community. Frollen was very instrumental in establishing the first college and public gymnasiums, for voluntary use, in America. Resigning at the close of the semester to take up other duties, Frollen was replaced by the third of Jahn's pupils, Francis Lieber (1800-1872). Lieber continued the gymnastics program at Harvard College until his acceptance by Columbia University as professor in the School of Law.

Gymnastics, through the efforts of Jahn's disciples, Beck, Frollen, and Lieber, spread throughout the United States. The first American *Turnverein* was established in 1848 in the city of Cincinnati; as the movement became increasingly popular the formation of the National *Turnerbund* (1850) came into being and the following year saw the beginning of the National *Turnfests* in Philadelphia at which time mass exhibitions in gymnastics were staged. The *Turnverein*, by 1851, boasted of a dozen associations including Kansas City, Chicago, Cleveland, and St. Louis, with a membership of over 10,000. It should be noted that the organization was not organized solely for the practice of gymnastics; the mental, social, religious and political aspects of life were also integrated parts of its total program.

Edward Hitchcock (1828–1911)

Amherst College, in 1861, under the direction of Dr. Hitchcock introduced the first significant program in gymnastics on the collegiate level. The 40′ x 50′ gymnasium housed apparatus as well as weights, stall bars, Indian clubs, and dumbbells. Each student was required to participate in one half hour of gymnastics four times per week.

Gymnastics in the United States
During Post-Civil War Years

Dioclesian Lewis (1823–1886)

Dio Lewis, a teacher of education, became engulfed in health and exercise when he strove to relieve his wife of tuberculosis. Being interested in the frail and uncoordinated, he set out to devise a gymnastic system that would enhance one's ability, gracefulness, flexibility and general health. In doing so, he openly opposed the German gymnastics system that predominantly developed musculature and strength and failed to significantly contribute to the old as well as the young; he also argued that it ignored females of all ages. (It should be assumed that he was referring to the German gymnastics system in the United States; for Spiess' system emphasized coeducational gymnastics.)

Lewis' system of gymnastics purported to serve all ages and all temperaments of both sexes. Calisthenics was the core of his program. His movements embodied many free exercises comprised of both resistive and non-resistive forces. His equipment was of a simple nature: Indian clubs, bean bags, wands, dumbbells, rubber balls, and wooden rings made of cherry wood. The rings were his favorite; the exercises consisted of antagonistic movements from hanging and supportive positions.

Being a thorough believer in the value of public relations, Lewis managed to give significant impetus to his programs during the trying Civil War years. Between 1860 and 1865, his system was introduced into the American schools. The exercises were of a free calisthenic nature and many of them could be executed while the students remained in their seats; the movements were performed on the average of 15 minutes per day. His teachings spread to the military and his program rapidly gained support for its contribution to the individual's physical, mental and moral culture.

Though the remnants of his teachings are few and far between, his major contributions still remain an integral part of our culture: gymnastics training for men, professional preparation for gymnastics teachers, and gymnastics in education.

A reemphasis of the *Turnverein* system came about after the retirement of Dio Lewis. A training school was erected in New York City where the German movement received new impetus.

George Brosius (1839–1920)

Brosius was appointed director of the training school when it moved to Milwaukee in 1947. Under his leadership the school inaugurated "medical" type gymnastics which emphasized an anatomical and physiological type of gymnastics. His revision also included a "school" gymnastics whose curriculum included terminology, progression, theory and practice, history and literature. This program added immensely to the caliber of gymnastic institutions, and before long, his *Turnverein* program was being successfully employed by the public schools. Many of the modern gymnastic programs are attributed to the leadership of Brosius.

Curriculum construction in gymnastics, as related to public education, was pioneered by Carl Betz (1854-1898), who formulated a series of gymnastics manuals that systemized the schools' apparatus program.

Hartvig Nissen (1835–1924)

Nissen was Vice-Consul for Norway and Sweden and in 1883 he was appointed head of the Swedish Health Institute in Washington, D. C. His application of Ling's system of gymnastics in Washington was very instrumental in promulgating the system throughout the United States.

As Swedish gymnastics became increasingly popular in the United States, its fundamental objectives were weighed against its effect on the body, both preventive and corrective, and by its artistic performance comprised of simplicity and ease of performance. The system proved itself worthy and was granted pedagogical merit. This sanction was instrumental in the success of the system's victory over Spiess' German techniques that were predominantly being employed in the Western part of the country; before long, the Ling system was either being employed in its entirety or contributing significantly as a variation—as was the case in the Sargent system of gymnastics training.

Dudley Allen Sargent (1849–1924)

Administrator of the Hemenway Gymnasium at Harvard College in 1879, Sargent introduced a system of gymnastics whose structure resembled Ling's medical gymnastics and whose basis was voluntary exercise based on an individual examination.

His system was characterized by a physical diagnosis which was followed by prescriptive exercises and diet control; the degree of intensity was determined by the individual physical needs. Sargent's interest in body symmetry was shown in his unique introduction of anthropometric measurements. The program's equipment included apparatus that was designed to provide resistive exercises to specific muscle groups by utilizing pulley weights and springs, in the form of sliding frames, treadles, and hand strengtheners. His anthropometric measurements determined one's body symmetry by accumulating such data as height of pubic arch and sternum, girth of the elbow and instep and the distance from the shoulder to the elbow.

Additional apparatus such as the parallel bars, horizontal bar, and side horses were employed for corrective as well as preventive purposes. Sargent's system, after becoming an integral part of Harvard's general education program, was adopted by many institutions of higher education throughout the New England area.

Thomas Dennison Wood (1865–1918)

It was his belief that the stereotyped and non-functional aspects of the German and Swedish gymnastics system would eventually become extinct.

At Leland Sanford University, Wood put his philosophy to work. Formal gymnastics was gradually replaced with natural and original types of activities (such as the racial activities of man) and the program adopted tumbling, a skill which up to this point had been regarded as circus activity. Apparatus activity was provided with a "pioneer" American educational touch. Complicated routines fixed by exact executions were replaced with a naturalism that established as its "set" routine, freedom of choice as viewed through primitive movements. While teaching at Columbia University, Wood named this pattern: Natural Gymnastics.

Young Men's Christian Association

The Y.M.C.A. and its affiliated International Training School (now Springfield College), in Massachusetts, were very influential in contributing to the growth of gymnastics in the United States. Utilizing the spiritual concept as its philosophical basis, the "Y," within a decade after its development in 1885, had established over 340 associations with a total of 140 physical education directors.

Robert McBurney (1837-1898), one of the first Association Secretaries (23rd Street Branch, New York City), played a significant role in promoting apparatus activity, when in 1887 he was instrumental in having the International Y.M.C.A. Commission adopt physical training in the school's training program.

Robert Jeffries Roberts (1849-1920) was appointed director of the newly created Physical Education Department at Springfield College. Under his direction and inspiration there was developed an "instrumental" and "pragmatic" type of gymnastics program—one that has carried over to the institution's present concept of instruction.

Luther Halsey Gulick (1865-1918) joined the physical education staff at Springfield College in the summer of 1887. The following year he became head of the department. His "primitive" and "natural" activity concept (that was originally formulated with his colleague Thomas Wood) of physical education was further injected into Springfield's program of instruction. Gulick, through the inspiration of Lawrence Doggett, Springfield's first president, believed that no barrier should exist between the religious and physical aspects of the school's program; this was confirmed when the college adopted his philosophic concept which is now the underlying philosophy of Springfield College and all Christian Associations throughout the world; *i.e.*, development of the whole man, spiritually, mentally, and physically. This triangular concept, which stresses an all-around personality and continuous growth through progressive programming, has enabled Springfield's students throughout the years to receive excellent preparation in gymnastics technique and also to become the nation's finest teachers, coaches, and administrators in the field of physical education.

World War I

Formal gymnastics was given new impetus in education during the years of World War I. The poor physical condition of the nation as a whole, as revealed by draft statistics, led the schools to concentrate on military training and physical fitness type programs of which formal gymnastics played a significant role. An important outgrowth of this fitness type program was a scientific movement; in the early twenties, a test and measurement program was incorporated in lieu of medical gymnastics. The features of this movement led to the development of achievement tests, achievement scales, use of statistical data and objective tests primarily concerned with motor performances.

Post World War I Years

The armistice of 1918 brought forth a re-evaluation of physical education. Emphasis was placed on mild recreation games; formal gymnastic activity remained popular only with minority groups. The populace, weary of the formality that accompanied military living, became very vulnerable to this mode of recreational programming. Stanley Hall, an enthusiast of the play and games movement stated, "play is the best kind of education, because it practices power of mind and body which, in our highly specialized civilization, would never otherwise have a chance to develop." Educators readily joined the play "band wagon" and started to include these types of activities in their physical education programs, which hitherto were comprised mainly of gymnastics. The athletic movement that gained prominence after the Civil War was also bidding for a "birth" in the schools' program. The National Association of Amateur Athletes of America, which in 1888 was named the Amateur Athletic Union (AAU), increased the popularity of sports throughout the nation. School systems started to integrate their gymnastics programs with indoor sports such as volleyball and basketball.

The inception of recreational and athletic programs in the physical education curriculum was indicative of a rising revolt against formalism in physical education. The outcome of this movement led state legislation (which established regulations for health and physical education) to shift emphasis away from formal gymnastics and calisthenics, for health and discipline, to favor the educational results of sports, games, athletics, and rhythmic activities (contrary to legislation passed prior to 1914 which made physical culture and calisthenics mandatory in the larger schools). Nationwide acceptance of this trend was apparent when in 1925, the National Federation of State High School Athletic Associations was formed. Previously, there was organized, in 1910, an athletic union in the form of the National Collegiate Athletic Association (NCAA). This organization tacked gymnastics to its roster in 1938.

As a separate entity, gymnastics could not compete with athletics in physical education and inevitably descended to one phase of the total program. The increased unpopularity of formal gymnastics in education received an additional "setback" from "Social Education," in the early thirties, which recognized the values of recreation in education, and "Educational Developmentalism" which was initiated in 1930 and has carried through to present times. "Everyone should be encouraged to take part regularly in a variety of activities appropriate to his age, physical condition, abilities and social interests"; "worthy use of leisure time" and "enrichment of human life" were slogans characteristic of these same educational philosophies.

Prior to World War II

Leslie J. Judd (1888–   )

A native of Collingwood, Victoria, Australia, and an expert performer in his own right, Mr. Judd has undoubtedly contributed more to the development of educational gymnastics than any other contemporary.

He received his professional training at Springfield College (Massachusetts); upon graduation, in 1920, he was appointed to the school's faculty as instructor of physical education. From the very onset of his teaching career, he exhibited professional mastery and dedication to physical education.

During the twenties and thirties, when sports and recreational activities became the mode of participation, Judd set out to give gymnastics a new and unique artistic dimension that later proved to be the main tie that helped to maintain the activity within the physical education curriculum. Through aesthetically appealing gymnastics skills,

Fig. 17: Leslie J. Judd

he established apparatus routines, dance selections, comedy antics, hand balancing acts, drills of various natures, including wand—Indian Club—and marching drills as well as his own "Living Statuary" or

"Tableaux." Several of his themes, namely "Aspiration," "Bondage and Freedom," and "Cooperation," have become classics in the field of physical education.

His exhibitional instructional program provided his students with the values that accompanied gymnastics training but his inclusion of a naturalism combined with rhythms produced activities that were not only enjoyable to the student, but also fun in nature combined with a sense of belonging that is so desirable to the American people. After organizing the Springfield College Exhibitional Team his aesthetic concept served as a significant link between gymnastics programs and public understanding of its values in education. Throughout the years his teams have been given international recognition, travelling extensively throughout the eastern part of the United States, Canada, and Mexico. His ideologies have been emulated by literally thousands of students that have passed through the West Gymnasium at Springfield and whose teachings extend to all the continents of the globe. Of primary importance was the fact that Judd did not place important emphasis on winning teams and successful exhibitions but rather on the total development of his individual students, a quality seldom accomplished at the present time.

Professor Judd's 33 years of unselfish and dedicated teaching and coaching has not for one moment gone unnoticed. In 1953 the West Gymnasium at Springfield College was dedicated the Leslie J. Judd Gymnasium; in 1955, he received the Norris Tarbell Medallion, the highest award offered by the Alumni Association of Springfield College for notable service to Alma Mater; and in 1958, he received the Helms Hall of Fame Award for noteworthy achievement in the promotion and teaching of gymnastics and most recently (1962) an honorary degree of doctor of humanities from Springfield College.

As a teacher, coach, and friend, Coach Judd has become known among his students and colleagues as the "Dean of American Gymnastics Coaches."

World War II and the Subsequent Years

World War II brought about a revival of past history; it reawakened educators to the fact that our growing youth requires programs of strenuous activity. This revival stemmed from the fact that physical examinations given to incoming service men indicated a deficiency in upper body strength, especially in the muscles of the shoulder girdle, the triceps, the abdomen, and the back. The reestablishment of physical fitness programs has gained additional support with the end of the Korean Conflict and the concept that man, being a biological creature, needs physical activities to offset the sedentary living that usually accompanies an "automotive existence."

Present Trend

The present trend in physical education is one of fitness of American youth. The program received major impetus from President John F. Kennedy, when he asserted:

> *The strength of our democracy is no greater than the collective well-being of our people. The vigor of our country is no stronger than the vitality and will of all our countrymen. The level of physical, mental, moral and spiritual fitness of every American citizen must be our constant concern.*

Upon the President's request, various educators tested many different activities to find which skills contributed to the physical fitness of the individual. Their findings revealed that the sport of gymnastics, when judiciously applied, scored very highly in the fitness area. These valid statistics have helped to bring about the reinstatement of gymnastics into the physical education program. However, progressive programming, which is the present mode of instruction, requires a relatively new concept of thought when dealing with an emancipated activity such as gymnastics.

Subject matter, which hitherto has been all-important, has become subdued and the child and his individual needs has taken precedence. This philosophical change in education has suppressed formal apparatus and has created the rise of an "artistic" type of gymnastics. Through aesthetically appealing gymnastic skills, educators are attempting to achieve a total fitness through the all-around program by developing the maximum potential within the individual, stressing consistency of performance and beauty of execution. The

Greek ideology of "inner and outer harmony of the body" is stressed through self-expression which comprises imagination, diligent work and concentration. Once the fundamental skills are attained the student is allowed freedom of improvisation which in turn helps to develop individual technique. Thus, we see the adoption of an "instrumental and pragmatic" philosophy of education very characteristic of the early training school in Springfield (Massachusetts) being utilized by the supporters of artistic gymnastics.

Today, gymnastics programs can be seen on all levels of education. The majority of state curriculum departments are prescribing no less than 10 percent of gymnastics to be included in primary and secondary physical education programs. In higher education, gymnastics is an integral part of the general education program as well as the professional curriculum.

The present trend in educational gymnastics received support from many dedicated teachers and coaches of physical education. The outcome of their individual initiative has significantly contributed to the over-all interest and success of apparatus activities throughout the nation. The prowess and leadership of a few of these individuals has served as a beacon in promoting gymnastics throughout the United States, e.g., the late Roy E. Moore, who dedicated himself for almost a half century to the betterment of the sport. During his lifetime he rose to the position of National A.A.U. and Olympic Gymnast Committee Chairman and Vice President of the International Gymnast Federation. While in office he served as a talisman to the many coaches and performers and in doing so promoted a unique type of goodwill for the sport, as well as for the A.A.U., as only Mr. Moore could have accomplished. Edward Scrobe, teacher of physical education in the New York City Public School System, and Lyle Welser, Gymnastics Coach at Georgia Tech., have both been very instrumental in contributing to the gymnastics program by their helping to formulate the National Gymnast Clinic (1954) in Sarasota, Florida. The general purpose of the clinic is to promote instructional and competitive interest in the activity. Since the clinic's formulation, Sarasota has become an annual trek for international gymnastics enthusiasts.

Gene Wettstone, Gymnastics Coach at Penn State University, an ardent supporter of educational gymnastics, has for years dedicated his teachings and leadership to the promotion of the activity. His colleagues, in recognizing his talents, elected him "Coach of the Year" in 1962 and the same group (National Association of Gymnastic Coaches) elected him to preside over their organization during that year.

It is obvious that the gymnastics pendulum is swinging into a new "Era of Enlightenment." History is repeating itself: it seeks to utilize the activity in the "Space Age" and at the same time help the individual to prepare for and to adjust to the complexities of a divided world.

Selected

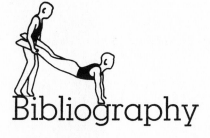

Bibliography

BOOKS

KUNZLE, G. C., *Olympia Gymnastic Series* (six books). London: James Barrie Books Ltd., 1957.*

LA PORTE, WILLIAM RALPH, and RENNER, A. G., *The Tumbler's Manual*. Englewood Cliffs, N.J.: Prentice-Hall, Inc., 1944.

LOKEN, NEWTON C. and WILLOUGHBY, ROBERT J., *Complete Book of Gymnastics*. Englewood Cliffs, N.J.: Prentice-Hall, Inc., 1959.

---

* Distributed by Sportsshelf, P.O. Box 634, New Rochelle, N. Y.

PRICE, HARTLEY D., HEWLETT, JOSEPH M., and LOKEN, NEWTON C., *Gymnastics and Tumbling* (rev.). New York: Ronald Press, 1950.

RYSER, OTTO, *Teacher's Manual for Tumbling and Apparatus Stunts* (second rev. ed.). Dubuque, Ia.: William C. Brown Co., 1951.

SCANNELL, JOHN, *A Manual of Heavy Apparatus and Tumbling Stunts.* Minneapolis: Burgess Publishing Co., 1956.

WEST, WILBUR D., *The Gymnast Manual,* Englewood Cliffs, N.J.: Prentice-Hall, Inc., 1942.

ZWARG, LEOPOLD F., *Apparatus and Tumbling Exercises.* Philadelphia: John Joseph McVey, 1923.

RESEARCH QUARTERLY

BROWN, HOWARD S. and MESSERSMITH, LLOYD, "An Experiment in Teaching Tumbling With and Without Motion Pictures," *Research Quarterly,* XIX (December 1948), pp. 304-307.

FIELD, DAVID A., "An Annotated Bibliography on Gymnastics and Tumbling," *Research Quarterly,* XXI (May 1950), pp. 112-125.

GERSHON, ERNEST, "Apparatus Gymnastics Knowledge Test for College Men in Professional Physical Education," *Research Quarterly,* XXVIII (December 1957), pp. 332-341.

SPENCER, RICHARD R., "Ballistics in the Mat Kip," *Research Quarterly,* XXXIV (May 1963), pp. 213-218.

THULIN, J. Q., *Gymnastic Handbook,* (Reviewed by C. H. McCloy for *Research Quarterly,* No. 4) Lund, Sweden: South Swedish Gymnastic Institute, 1947.

Index

239